BROKEN

BROKEN

Making Sense of Life After Your Parents' Divorce

TIM BAKER

THINK

TH1NK
P.O. Box 35001
Colorado Springs, Colorado 80935

TH1NK is an imprint of NavPress.

ISBN 1-57683-653-3

Cover design by studiogearbox.com
Cover photo by Jonathan Andrew/Corbis
Creative Team: Nicci Hubert, Amy Spencer, Kathy Mosier, Arvid Wallen, Angie Messinger

**Published in association with the literary agency of Alive Communications, Inc.,
7680 Goddard Street, Suite 200, Colorado Springs, Colorado 80920
(www.alivecommunications.com).**

Baker, Tim, 1965-
  Broken : making sense of life after your parents' divorce / Tim Baker.
    p. cm.
  ISBN 1-57683-653-3
  1. Baker, Tim, 1965- 2. Christian biography. 3. Children of divorced parents—Religious
life. I. Title.
  BR1725.B3318A3 2006
  248.8'6—dc22

                                               2005037601

Printed in the United States of America

1 2 3 4 5 6 7 8 9 10 / 10 09 08 07 06

FOR A FREE CATALOG OF NAVPRESS BOOKS & BIBLE STUDIES,
CALL 1-800-366-7788 (USA) OR 1-800-839-4769 (CANADA)

For my brother and sister

CONTENTS

ACKNOWLEDGMENTS

THANKS,

. . . *Jesus*.

. . . My parents. I love you.

. . . Jacqui, for wading through my emotions and listening to me vent and letting me cry through long hours of writing. You have endured more than anyone I know. You are my best thing. I love you.

. . . Nicole, Jessica, and Jacob, for letting go of me for a bit to write this book. You are perfect children. I don't care how that sounds to the people who read that and think I'm exaggerating. You really are perfect. I love you.

. . . Nicci Hubert, Andrea Christian, and my Nav / TH1NK friends. Thanks for believing in me, for taking a chance with this project, and for loving me to the deadline.

. . . To you, for reading this book. I hope it begins something good in you.

BROKEN THINGS

NO ONE SEEMS TO WANT broken things.

I know this because I've seen Dumpsters filled with broken toys and torn coats and ripped-open pillows thrown in with half-eaten sandwiches and old milk cartons. Broken things do not serve useful purposes and they do not help advance society and they are not the kind of thing you want to have around. No one goes shopping for broken things. No one gives broken things as gifts.

I wonder if broken things have their own private story about their lives as loved and unbroken things. Could a broken and discarded toy tell a story about the day he was unwrapped and played with and cherished? Would he speak of those days with that certain sparkle in his eye, the kind of a sparkle that shows how much those unbroken days meant to him? Would those old shoes gathering dust in your closet tell stories about that last hike or the time you kissed your date good night for the first time?

People crave unbroken things. Do things crave to be unbroken? Do people?

What about those of us who were the bright and shiny gift someone's eyes sparkled over as she held us in a blanket and presented us with pride and hope before the church or grand-mother or best friend? At least to someone, at some point, we were hoped for. And then that thing happened to us—our parents divorced or abused us or abandoned us, and ultimately broke us. Now do people want us?

Who would? Broken toys are tossed aside. Used wrappers are thrown away. Broken people are discarded too. I know this because I've seen people left in their brokenness, discarded by their parents, their friends, or the people who loved them the most. Discarded because they were "too broken." Discarded because that's what you do with broken things.

After my parents divorced, I felt psycho-weird-strange-abnormal; I felt like I had rabies all the time or like I was psychotically depressed on the inside or like I couldn't laugh without knowing I was going to have to cry alone afterward. It sucks being broken, like that thing that can't be fixed, like that thing no one wants. No one wants a broken thing. Sometimes it feels like no one wants a broken me.

LAYERS

I'm not entirely sure how we're supposed to learn about brokenness, and I'm not sure how we're supposed to get to the place of being more healed. I don't know how to make God notice that I'm still not totally fixed, that I want to be healed and whole again, and that I want to be able to praise him honestly for who I am and what he made me to be.

Maybe God doesn't just wave his hand or make a declaration of healing. Maybe it's something I have to journey through. Possibly, the journey is the healing process that God has designed. To be honest, I'm not sure.

I guess it's a choice—like a life choice. We can stay here and stay broken, or we can move ourselves forward and, fueled by the desire to be whole again, we can begin learning what it means to be unbroken.

My best way of understanding it is like this: We have to organize our lives into layers, taking each layer and living it again. We start with the layer that represents when we were born, or the earliest layer we can remember. And then the next layer. And then the next.

Imagine each of these layers set out before you on a table. They sit there like a pile of thin tissue paper, each page different from the others. You take the first layer and study its texture, color, and size. You go through the process of hating that layer, then understanding it, then loving it, then embracing it as who you are.

Each layer has to be understood and loved differently. Some layers we can deal with quickly. Other layers will take years to learn, understand, and accept.

JOURNEY

The worst part of reliving those layers is, we often can't remember many of the early ones. They're there, but some memories, like old, faded photographs, are hard to make out clearly. Now and then we catch an old memory floating through. We can barely make out the characters in the picture or tell what the subject is.

Sometimes these old memories are out of focus. Often they are woven together. Awful moments combine to make an awful family memory. The problem with these memories is that the ones that come to the surface are often the worst ones, or they're fake ones. You know those fake ones, I'm sure. They're the ones you create in your mind to compensate for missing or really awful memories.

Looking through these layers of old memories is a long process. Maybe this is the way God wants it. Is he watching us study and learn and accept? Is he holding us while we search through those layers? Is he taking each one off, only when we're ready? I don't know. But I believe in God, and I know he's real. I figure he doesn't want us to stay broken.

Each layer leads us closer to understanding how our parents' divorce pulled us apart and made us feel like something lying with the old banana peels and the rest of the stinking trash. Looking at each layer helps us realize that God is putting us back together, piece by piece. He's showing us that we don't belong in the trash; even though we felt trashed, we were never really there. Life broke us, but we are not ruined. God puts us back together, and he does it slowly because if he did it all at once, I imagine we'd probably explode.

HOPE

This feels like good news. Like *the* good news.

We stand broken before God, and he does not look past our brokenness. He sees our broken souls and spirits and our hurting hearts. In this physical world, where we often bump meaning-lessly into each other, ignoring each other's hurt and pain, God does not do that.

He sees.

He knows.

He seeks out.

He heals.

Hope isn't about trusting psychologists, medications, or any other man-made healing tactic. Hope is built on what God has done for us and others in the past. It is built on knowing what God has done and trusting that he'll continue doing that, even for and in *us*. So we hope that God will heal us, but that's not like the hope we have that today's mail will bring a check for a thousand dollars or the kind of hope we have for better weather. This is an unusual hope. A certain hope.

We trust God because he promises healing. We trust him because he does heal.

He heals us. Even broken us.

MIRACLE

And that healing is a miracle.

The truth of God in us is this: Divorce might break us, but we do not have to remain broken. Even though our lives are damaged, God makes that damage a miracle. Even though our lives feel beyond repair, God repairs.

This miracle is a *possible* miracle. The miracle of being healed from divorce often feels like we're asking God to reattach a severed limb, but I imagine that to God it is as easy as replacing a lightbulb.

Part of the miracle of God's healing is the actual healing. Another part is watching it happen. We do not sit idly by and wait while wearing a blindfold. We get to watch God working in us.

There is pain in our parents' divorce, but there is also a hefty miracle. This is that miracle: God loves us, reaches inside us, and reshapes what divorce wrecked. Only God can do this and, truth is, God's the only one who really wants to do it. Want, combined with ability—that is God's miracle healing in us.

So we reach through the layers. We discover the memories. We relearn who we are. We uncover the beautiful thing God made us to be, that thing buried under the yuck of the pain. And in the process, we become again what God planned all along. His healed child living whole-ly for him.

This is our life-process.

It begins now.

Here we are, God. Heal us.

ONE

MEMORIES

IF SHOES MAKE THE MAN, then Vans sneakers are the kind of man I am. I'm forty, and I don't race bikes anymore. I've never been on a skateboard and I'm not really cool enough to wear my Vans. Still, these sneakers are my connection to the old me. I wore Vans when I was a kid. I wore them before the divorce. And I love them like I love my childhood.

I need that connection because I have forgotten so much of what I have lived through. Even though it feels like a completely empty attempt, if I keep wearing these shoes I will always have my childhood with me somehow. It makes sense if you think about it. Shoes aren't memories, but they make me feel like I have memories.

Memories of our childhood go in two directions. There are the memories we can remember: good or bad times during our childhood that we easily recall. Then there are those memories we can't recall: good or bad missing moments. This can be agonizing. If we don't remember our childhood, how can we know what we were like?

Whatever our memories, remembering is important—reaching back and rediscovering what we can remember, and searching for

what we can't remember. The journey toward understanding the
layers of who we are begins with journeying into the past. We need
our memories. We need to remember who we used to be. Before
the before. Back when things were as God intended. If we choose
not to remember and if we choose not to deal with our memories,
we won't understand why we act or feel the way we do right now.
We have to face our memories so we can live our future.

■ ■ ■

My memories.

Southern California smells like fresh flowers and saltwater and
coconut suntan lotion.

Everywhere I go there are people in bathing suits. There are
sandcastles and ice-cream trucks with kids crowded around. Everyone eats out all the time—fast-food tacos or Jack in the Box. Kids
spend all day with their parents or friends. They build forts in
trees or wage wars against invisible armies or race bikes up and
down the street. Or they spend all day at the beach. They party
and they play and they do not hurt.

Our family of five exists as part of the Southern California culture. We are good like everyone else. We eat at Jack in the Box
like they do. We go to the beach and build sandcastles and crowd
around the ice-cream man. We have many cool friends who race
things and ride things and cook out a lot. My older brother, my
younger sister, and I spend our days in our huge Southern California backyard.

There's the tree fort that I helped my brother and his friend
build. We listened to Alice Cooper's "School's Out" over and over

as we hammered and sweated, created and sawed, and built on to our mom's favorite avocado tree. She said it was okay, and we hated avocados anyway. Many people stayed in our fort, but our most memorable guests were several thousand bees that swarmed from a neighbor's hive.

In the garage, we and several other kids from the block put on a last-minute Halloween play and horror house. There was a magic show, a few performances, and this one part where we used cooked spaghetti and olives to make people believe they had their hands in a pot of brains and eyeballs. There's the driveway, where I learned how to ride my green Schwinn without training wheels. Not too long after that, I learned that the metal poles on my seat made sparks on the driveway. I learned to pop wheelies and make hard turns just so I could make those sparks. I like to think there are scrapes from the metal on that driveway right now.

If you'd asked me when I was six if there was another world out there beyond Southern California, I would have said no. If you had asked me if any place smelled sweeter or if there was any other way of existing on this planet, I would have said no. That's because there really wasn't any other way of existing. Not when you're six. Where you're living ought to smell sweet. And your parents are your security. If you had asked me when I was six, I would have told you how secure and strong and protecting my parents were. I might have told you, in my own six-year-old way, that my parents were my world. They were my anchor. My compass.

I miss Southern California and I miss my childhood. I hate that my childhood was wrecked by divorce. I hate that I have this story to tell.

I wish I was still six years old.

Memory Warehouse

Sometimes it feels like all our memories are kept locked up in a huge warehouse. We each have our own warehouse, a large room filled with aisles of shelves, each aisle representing a different experience. There are aisles that represent a favorite house. Aisles filled with memories of family vacations. Aisles packed with good memories. Aisles loaded with bad memories. And we continually walk those aisles, searching for and remembering our past.

If you had the chance to shop for your memories, which aisle would you shop in? Would you stand in the aisle where you learned to ride a bike? Would you walk the aisle where you and your brother were still together? Would you visit the aisle where your family was actually happy, whole, and healthy?

See, most of us have great memories of our families, and most of us have very bad memories too. They're all in there, locked up in that memory warehouse. Even when we have the opportunity to look around the warehouse, we often choose to stand in only one aisle of memories.

But if we don't look around, searching through all our memories, good and bad, we get locked into only one perspective about who our family is. Some of us recall only memories of our family drama. We easily recall those moments when our parents constantly yelled. We recall our abuse. We recall the agony of our parents' divorce. But when we stand only in that aisle of negative memories, those memories become our identities. We become perpetually hurting people who will never get through our parents' divorce.

Others of us choose to recall only good memories. Yeah, there are rows of negative moments in our lives, but we shop along as if we can't see them. We choose to walk around good memories of steamy Christmas meals and chilly ski trips. But by only recalling the positive moments, we become always positive but secretly unhappy and internally conflicted. Our insides are confused because we know there's more to our memories than we are choosing to remember.

Still others of us would love to recall all of our memories, but we can't. We'd love to walk more than just the three aisles of memories we constantly walk; we know those other memories are there. But those aisles are barricaded, lined with huge guys holding grenades and machine guns. Those memories are locked up because someone in our family doesn't want us walking those aisles. Walking them gets us into trouble or attacked.

And then there are the aisles I walk, and maybe you walk these too. We walk only a few rows of memories because they are the only rows we're aware of. We are missing many memories. They're absent, removed, burned. Whatever happened, somehow we can't find them. So we constantly recall the few memories we have, reliving every last moment. Maybe a new memory is added once in a while. And when a new one is added, we cherish it and relive it. Doesn't matter if it's a good or a bad memory either.

Shopping for memories is that thing we need to do, that thing that often feels impossible. Some of us want to shop, but looking for new memories is painful. We desperately want to seek out more of who we are and learn to look into our families and remember, but that remembering feels awful.

GOD AND MEMORIES

There among those stacks, rows, and shelves of memories, God wanders around recalling the things he's watched us live through. There among all those moments that make up our identities, God looks over our history and sees the times he lovingly acted on our behalf and the times he lovingly didn't act. I imagine God wandering among my own memory-filled shelves, recalling and laughing and weeping and celebrating. I know God does that because throughout Scripture he reminds people of their history. This is the same God who knew Moses' childhood pain and his murdering past. This is the same God who knew about Paul's hatred for the church and his pious religious past. This is the same God who knows your aisles, your forgotten memories.

God was there at your family vacations. When your parents divorced. The time you hit your brother. God was present for all of those moments. They are an ever-present reality for him because he loves you. He was there when you were hurting and he was there when you celebrated.

This is tough theology. Tough because some of us would rather there were moments that God didn't see—those private sins or moments so personal we wouldn't want anyone to see them, including God. Especially God. It's tough because we often want to hide from God. Yeah, we want him to know about our hurts and pains, but only those we're comfortable with him seeing.

And it's tough because if God saw and knew and was present, why didn't he stop the bad things from happening? He knew what was happening in our parents' marriage, so why didn't he make it better? God saw that they were splitting and that the split was

going to break us, so why weren't we protected? If God didn't protect us, can he truly love us? Anyone or anything that claims to
love has to have within it the capacity to protect. That protection
has to be a part of that love. If God truly loves us, wouldn't he be
willing to shield us from those painful memories he knows about?

Could it be that God has a greater purpose, idea, or plan for
us and that purpose will now be fulfilled as a result of our parents'
divorce? Is there something in God's plan for our futures that
means we have to first remember all our past hurts before we can
move forward?

ABSENT MEMORIES

Some of us actually walk the aisles of memories and don't remember much. We have this idea that there are certainly more aisles,
but we can't find them. If you've lived through this, you understand how agonizing it is.

Psychologists will tell you a variety of reasons why many of
us don't remember our childhoods. Some believe memories are
blocked by traumatic experiences. Others believe we choose to
forget because our memories are hurtful or because we don't feel
comfortable focusing on negative experiences. Whatever the reason, we often don't remember, and not remembering all of who we
used to be can be excruciating.

This is called stress-induced amnesia. When we experience
trauma—a car accident, seeing someone killed, living through
divorce—those stress-filled experiences stop our mental processes
and cause us to forget everything. If that event hadn't been so
traumatizing, we might remember more. For those of us who don't

remember much about our lives since our parents divorced, that's amnesia working.

Stress doesn't just make us forget. It also causes us to make up fantastic stories and memories about our families—things that never happened. Our parents fighting over who has to pick up groceries becomes a new story: "Mom and Dad beat each other up because neither wanted to feed us." Mom and Dad having one good meal together with the family transforms into a fairy tale: "We were the happiest family."

Sometimes we don't remember, or we remember our past in a skewed way, because we're told to remember it that way. Some of our families make it taboo to remember anything about our lives together as a happy family; bringing up a joyful memory is met with a "we don't talk about those things anymore" message. Some of us remember our family as a wrecked thing, yet other people have told us that our family was really wonderful. Confusing. And the same can work in the opposite direction. Some of our families want to have only good memories. When we talk about a bad memory, our family insists it never happened.

Aching Memories

Some of us are haunted by the memories of our families. We remember everything: details about vacations, particulars about Christmas dinners and Thanksgiving meals and all those good times spent together. And now that our parents are divorced, those memories mock us. We are constantly reminded about what we lost. It's always there telling us that we once were whole.

It hurts. It's an aching memory.

The cruelest part of these memories is that we can't help but relive them. We want so bad to have our families back that we'll gladly walk those aisles over and over, searching for what went wrong and for details we don't ever want to forget—moments that are beautiful and that we can cherish.

It's important to embrace that ache. It's okay to celebrate what we used to have. God wants us to embrace those things, even the hard things. They make us who we are. And they link us back to life before our parents divorced, which is an important part of the healing process.

REMEMBERING BEFORE THE BEFORE

The moment my parents split, a new me was created. From that moment forward, all of my identity was formed and fashioned subconsciously by the fact that I came from a divorced family.

Because our identity can shift like that, remembering ourselves before our parents' divorce is essential. But what happens if we genuinely can't remember *anything* about our childhood? Or, even worse, what happens if all of what we remember is terrible? Some of us were older and we have a clear understanding of who we were and what life was like before the divorce. Others of us remember, and what we remember is too rough. Or we had no clue—or if we had a clue, it's been long forgotten.

Because I had forgotten a lot of my past, my beginning point always felt like it was in flux. I knew that I was born, but I barely remembered anything about my family; it was always that great unknown. The key for me was in finding old family photographs.

One day I came across this old picture of me when I was about nine years old. I was wearing werewolf fangs and had werewolf hair glued to my face. Dime-store fake blood dribbled out of my mouth, like I had just sucked the blood out of the photographer, who had taken the picture as lasting proof that werewolves do exist. That picture became my link to Kid Tim. It opened a door. I searched for more pictures.

Finding them was not easy. We had moved a lot, so locating the right box with the right pictures became a several-year journey. The more I looked, the more I realized that my family didn't take a lot of pictures after the divorce. Maybe pictures reminded us of too much pain. I'm not sure.

One summer, I was searching in Mom's house and found a box filled with slides of me and my family. Those slides told the tale of my childhood: I did smile when I was a kid. We did take vacations. There was joy and happiness.

I stole as many pictures as I could.

That same year, my wife had some of these slides transferred into real photographs and gave them to me on my birthday. I remember opening that photo album and looking at those pictures. I remember crying as I really looked at who I was as a kid: I had blond hair. I had an excited smile. I had big brown eyes. I loved to make stupid faces and do stupid things just so whoever looked at that picture would look at me. I was a hellion and a handful. I was me.

It felt so good to meet *me*.

It's good and right and healthy to remember. Before we think about our parents' divorce, we have to consider those good times that are long past. We were happier. We were healthier. For many of us, there was love and family and togetherness. Some members of our family might not like us remembering those times, but that doesn't mean we never lived them.

Remembering only part of our story is like beginning a good novel in the middle. The story does not make sense, we don't fully know the characters, and the ending feels disconnected and contrived.

WHAT DO WE DO WITH THIS?

The first important step on our journey out of brokenness begins with prayer. I'm going to suggest prayer many times throughout this book, because prayer acknowledges the ever-present help of God. We have to pray because we have to communicate with him, the Healer, if we want to become truly healed. So we implore God to begin this journey with us.

We pray . . .

"God, please walk my aisles."
We say this because inviting God to walk through our memories is the best way to start. When we say this we are really saying, "God, I am surrendering all of my memories to you. I surrender what I remember and I surrender what I don't remember. I want you to reveal what I don't currently remember but that you want me to know."

"God, please walk my aisles with me."
Inviting God to look into our memories isn't all we have to do. I imagine that God wants to walk with us. Can you imagine what that might be like, if that could really happen? It'd be like wandering

through your grandmother's closet with her and taking the time to let her tell you all the stories she remembers about each object: the shawl Grandpa gave her, those shoes she wore to the ball. I imagine God doing the same thing. He'd pick up our memories and remark often: "Ohhh yeah. I remember that. Coke spewed all out of your nose. I laughed." And "Suuurre! I remember that shirt. You wore it when that girl tried to kiss you. Yeah, made me kinda queasy too." God is personal and he is present. Those moments aren't at all out of character with who he is.

"God, please take these memories."
It's important to take the most awful and painful memories, look them over, and then place them in God's shopping cart. These memories are the ones we need divine help with. We place them in God's cart, but that's not the last we see of them. These are the ones God brings back at just the right moment so we can deal with them and be healed through them.

"God, please fill these shelves."
We need to ask God to fill the empty shelves where we know our crucial memories belong. We might ask him to replace them or to help us recall them. This is what I'd say to God, but I wouldn't just say it. I'd probably demand it. I'd be adamant. I'd want my memories.

SURRENDER

I've always imagined that moments with God wouldn't be spent singing or bowing or hovering in his presence. Moments with

God would be spent cuddling in his lap. I can't imagine any other posture. Maybe lying there, we'd sing to him, quietly, in a whisper. Maybe we would whisper one stanza of an old hymn and between each stanza he'd whisper-sing back, "I love you, oh how I love you," melodically and right in tune and step with the hymn we're singing to him.

When I think about surrendering to God, that's the posture I imagine taking. And in his presence and in that posture, I would do this, and I hope you'd agree that you'd do this too: I'd surrender to God all those awful memories. I would say to him out loud all of my painful memories and all of my happy memories. I would confess my anger at not remembering all of my childhood. I would say everything. I would say everything because I can. I would say everything because he wants me to.

We can say to God how we long to be able to walk all of the aisles of all of our memories. God wants to be involved. So here, at the beginning, we have to invite him into the process. And we should want God involved. Whether our memories hurt or not, whether they're pleasant or painful, we need God smack in the middle of our memory aisles.

God is wandering the aisles of your heart. He's wandering your memories. He's dying for you to invite him into the journey from being broken to being whole.

T W O

HEROES

I AM A PRETTY NORMAL kid.

Saturday-morning cartoons are my world, and this Saturday is a lot like last Saturday and that Saturday was a lot like the one before. There is a weird kind of consistency and normalcy to my world. Dad goes to work every morning. He comes home at night and smells hot and sweaty, like the air-conditioning wasn't on that day and he forgot his deodorant. He kisses Mom hello and heads for the dinner table.

I remember one night in particular, when Dad snapped at me because I had an imaginary friend who kept beating me up.

"Can I get some more milk, Dad?"

"Sure," he says.

I head for the fridge and almost make it, and then my imaginary friend kicks my legs out from under me and my plastic cup goes flying onto the stove.

"Tim, you better stop it, Son. You better stop it right now," Dad says.

I get up and make it to the fridge, fill my glass, and head back to my seat. I'm in my seat for a few seconds before my imaginary friend smacks me on the side of the head and knocks me into my sister.

Dad sends me to my room. I feel cared for, disciplined, complete.

On one particular Saturday, filled with completeness and cartoons, the normal repetitive security of my tiny world changes.

Mom sits on one side of the table where we have just eaten our cereal. Dad sits directly opposite her.

I remember a lot of laughing. Not the kind of laughing you hear after a good joke or when you nail someone with a water balloon. More like the nervous kind of laughing you might hear at a funeral or at the bedside of someone trying to be funny in the emergency room. The kind of laughter manufactured to cover up emotions you're not ready to deal with.

To be honest, I have no idea what the words were. Maybe this is one of those protecting things our minds do when we've experienced something too painful. The idea was pretty clear:

Moving out.

Taking stuff.

Won't be back for a while.

It's a pretty nice apartment.

Mom is smiling. The curlers in her hair pull her eyes back, making her look Chinese. I hear Scooby-Doo in the background. I want to go wrap myself in it.

"Okay," I say, feeling my face go blank. What kind of expression should I have? Should I make a speech? Maybe I should throw myself on the floor, and scream and cry, and blame it on my imaginary friend. Really I don't know what to do. How do you respond to your world falling apart?

That night, with our house decorated for Thanksgiving and with us in our pajamas, Dad begins packing his car. Bags and boxes and memories and emotions. He's making trips to his car, and I'm wondering how much he's taking with him. There's a saturation point to all of this. If he takes just a little, that means he'll be back for more stuff, or he'll have less stuff to bring back with him. If he takes everything, this move is for good. Permanent.

He takes everything. I want my Scooby-Doo. I want Mom's curled hair. I want my imaginary friend to come and beat me up and add some comedy. I want Dad to yell at me. I'd even take a spanking if it meant he'd stay for a few more minutes. Too bad my gentle dad rarely spanks.

Our family gathers in the den. At first, no one cries. No one laughs. We just stare. And then, one at a time my brother, my sister, and I begin to weep. All of us want to go. All of us cling to him. I can still feel his leg under my two-armed grip.

He waves good-bye and drives away. Dad is gone. He'll never be home again.

I'm sure some of us ran to our rooms and cried there too. I remember feeling helpless and crying out that helpless feeling. There, out the door, went my heart and my dad and my future. And nothing I could do would stop that.

I've always wondered if Mom cried herself to sleep that night. I wonder if Dad cried. I wonder if God did.

Yet I don't care if Mom or Dad or even God cried. My heart broke and my insides bled. My stomach opened and my veins turned to water and my blood did too. Everything that happened that holiday night changed everything about who I was and who I would be. The rest of me, all of me, changed when my parents split up. I was not the same after that night. And because of that night I will always be half a person in a land of whole people. I am now not who I was supposed to be.

I was angry. Pissed is really a better word. At first that anger felt completely wrong and yet completely right. I felt I had a right to be angry with my parents, and at the same time I felt shame for being angry with them. How dare I get angry with my parents? They gave me life; they raised me, fed me, cared for me. But they also broke me.

Why do people who love you tear your heart out? How can people who love you do unloving things to you? This isn't discipline, like a spanking or needing to learn a hard lesson. Sometimes the people you love leave, and that's just the way it is. That's what I learned that night. All my crying and all my holding on and all my begging didn't make my parents stay married.

I failed.

What We Don't Think About

You know, there's a world that's happening right around us, and we often don't even notice it. Like the world that our parents are living in. Their relationship. Their together times. Their quiet times when they're alone together in the car or in the bedroom or in the hallway just outside the dining room. Their private conversations, the adult kind, the ones we'd never understand as kids. While we are totally unaware of what's happening around us, they're working out finances and saving for vacations. They're thinking through the family schedule and planning who's taking who to soccer practice.

We aren't aware of this world, but it exists just as surely as you are holding this book. And in their world—your parents' world—their relationship existed completely outside your family. Your parents knew each other before you were living. Their relationship spans further back than the beginning of your life. They dated. Your dad looked into your mom's eyes and thought she was wonderful. Your mom looked into your dad's eyes and imagined spending the rest of her life with him.

Relationships—good ones—don't happen overnight. Divorce doesn't happen overnight either. It's that whole iceberg thing. Whatever you were seeing in your parents' relationship was only one very small part of it. There was a whole lot more going on under the surface. The angst and anger and fighting might very possibly have been an old thing for them. It's just something you didn't often think about.

Maybe looking at divorce from our perspective isn't always the best way to look at divorce. Maybe trying to look at it from our parents' perspective is better. And maybe, in doing that, we understand that, while our parents' divorce feels awful, it probably has been on its way to happening for a long time.

INSTINCT

Maybe it would be better if I called this section "Coping Mechanisms." Or I could call it "The Ways We Freak Out When Our Parents Divorce." We do freak out, and we do so because what is happening is 100 percent unnatural.

Here our brains help us out a lot. We can reason through understanding this split and say that because of our parents' divorce we are experiencing extreme emotional trauma. That's fairly intellectual and heady. But what we experience isn't reason. We don't react to what's happening in our families with pure, untouched cognitive regularity like a mechanic or an accountant. Divorce pulls our hearts apart, and our response to that trauma is naturally emotional.

Maybe emotions aren't the best thing to rule us when our parents divorce, but it's natural that they do. My mind can reason through why parents divorce, and I can think through the appropriate responses to the event. But none of us lives in that perfect cognitive state where we react logically. No, we respond to that emotional punch by compensating.

Some of us compensate by moving inside ourselves. We make up an internal world where we're most secure. This inside world doesn't include many people, and those it does include are people who live inside too. We do not go out. We do not have many, if any, true friends. We do not let people know what's happening to our insides. We are private.

We create our life this way because it's an instinctual reaction to not having control over what's happening to our outside world. Living a tiny life on the inside means we can live and be happy in our tiny space where our parents' divorce doesn't hurt. But living inside doesn't work, because it doesn't deal effectively with the pain or with the process of the divorce. Truthfully, all it does is block us off from the outside world, where people wait to help us with what we're feeling.

We also compensate when we use substances. We think drugs or alcohol or something else will make us feel better. But if you numb the pain you only open the door to loads of other problems.

Alcohol and drugs kill your body. Too much food makes you fat and unhealthy, and more food makes you even more depressed and unbalanced. In compensating with substances, you never really deal with what's actually happening in life. Further, you lose the ability to deal with any pain in the future. Maybe using substances makes that awful pain feel better, but what about the next awful thing? You can never eat or drink or do drugs enough to get away from pain permanently. In the end you wind up fat, drunk, sad, or dead.

Rather than using drugs or food, some of us compensate for our parents' split by trying to fill ourselves up on love. We find love from those who say they love us but then use us, or we find love from those who are more needy than we are.

It's natural for us to look for people who will love us. It's also natural for us to seek physical comfort. This compensating tactic doesn't work, though, because it replaces our need to be comforted from our parents' divorce with a desire to be sexually satisfied. The result is that we get sexual gratification confused with pain and the need to be healed. Love-compensators often find themselves at the end of a string of physical relationships without ever having any real relationships and without ever finding hope or healing.

We also compensate by using anger. When anger stems from a divorce, it's often because that person is still hurting from the breakup or choosing not to accept it. Because anger-compensators choose not to deal with their parents' divorce, they are often mean and hateful. It's more fun to be stuck in an elevator with a pile of horse poop than to be around one of these people. Anger-compensators end up alone in life, living bitterly and angrily through their existence.

And we compensate when we act like we don't give a crap. If

we can act like what's happening isn't affecting us, if we can imagine that our parents' divorce doesn't hurt, if we can convince ourselves and our friends that the divorce doesn't really matter, then we believe that in some cosmic way we won't really hurt and the pain will go away. We may not be able to get our parents back together, but we can cheat our way out of that awfulness by acting like we are not hurting.

This one's effective because everyone loves a strong person. Everyone loves a hero. So you can stick your chest out, walk with a bit of an attitude, and live like what's happening doesn't even register with you. And if you live it just right, people will actually think you've dealt with what happened. They'll believe you're as strong as you think you are. They'll think you're superhuman. But acting like you don't care is awful, because nothing really gets accomplished. In the end, all you end up doing is looking cool but aching inside because you've alienated any remote possibility of getting help and healing.

A SPRINT FOR RESCUE

I get the whole compensating thing. Whether we think about it or not, when our parents divorce we all instinctually want to find a way to heal ourselves. But acting on that instinct and using whatever compensation it leads us to is almost always destructive. Filling ourselves up with human love, substances, and anger, and firewalling ourselves from the rest of the world are irrational solutions. They feel rational, but they're not. The only rational thing to do is to sprint toward something bigger than us and our situation and our pain. Our situation is awful, and we need rescue.

I've always believed that God is the only one who can truly rescue me from my parents' divorce. I think that's because the pain has always been too deep, and nothing else has ever seemed to fully heal me. I know that God can't stand it when we're hurting and I know that he longs to heal us. I guess that first step toward being healed from the moment our parents divorce is sprinting to God, grasping his feet, and begging him to heal us.

RELEASE THE PAST

I had an infected tooth once that was giving me a lot of trouble. The pain was excruciating. It was the kind of pain that doesn't just stay in the tooth; it tightened my jaw and made my whole head ache. Luckily I was able to get an appointment with the dentist on pretty short notice. I don't enjoy going to the dentist, but in this case it really didn't matter. The dentist was the only person who could heal me.

All it took was a simple X-ray to get the really bad news: I needed a root canal. The infection and decay had spread through the entire tooth, into the root, and was nearing the jawbone. The dentist agreed to work on it that very day. There were several shots of Novocain, lots of drilling, some filing down into the roots of my tooth. Blood. Goo. You get the idea.

When the dentist began releasing the infection in my tooth, my jaw felt better immediately. Yet I didn't know how incredibly good the tooth would feel until after the Novocain and pain from the process wore off. The only very negative part of that process, other than the pain of the drilling and the thought of someone drilling into my tooth, was the horribly nasty smell of the infection as it was being sucked out.

I remember thinking to myself that my rotten tooth was still functional and I could have gone on using my mouth for as long as I could stand the pain. But it was the pain that led me to the dentist. Yeah, I could have functioned at whatever capacity I could endure, but I would not have been operating completely. I would have had to compensate with my chewing. I would have had to constantly rub the side of my jaw, trying to work the pain and spread it out. I would have had to take a lot of aspirin to trick my body into thinking there really wasn't any pain. I would have had to continue coming up with a hundred little coping mechanisms if I wanted to continue ignoring my need for help. Those ways to cope aren't really living, and they're not really doing anything to heal the disease in my tooth.

For much of my own life, I have created little compensating tactics for dealing with my parents' divorce. I don't have to deal with what happened, really; I can just find another way of living. If I can effectively hide how I feel or numb the pain, then I'm doing just fine. Really.

That's no way to live, because in there, inside us, is anger and pus and hurt and goo, and after too long we start to stink.

I want you to begin doing something. I want you to begin giving up to God all the anger and pain you recall or feel from your parents' divorce. Those coping mechanisms you've probably created aren't really working. If your friends were being honest with you, they'd probably say they can smell your hurt for miles. If those who love you would be honest, you'd probably hear that they'd love it if you'd take some time and look back.

GOD'S OPEN ARMS

Can I introduce you to the one part of God that we rescue-sprinters need at this point? This is the part of God we often refer to in our discussions of our lives, and we often hear about these attributes of God when we're listening to sermons or Bible studies. We know about these qualities of God, but they're also the ones we all too often choose not to embrace.

This is God:

God to the Egyptian-slave Israelites: "I will free you."

God to the always-spiritually-adulterous Israelites: "Please stop messing up; I love you too much for that."

God to the Israelites in captivity: "I know where you are."

Jesus with the little children: "Let them come to me."

Jesus with the Gentiles, the outsiders: "I have come for you too."

Jesus with the lame, broken, blind, possessed: "I will heal you."

Jesus to John socked in on Patmos, writing to broken churches: "I am coming back for you."

Do you know the part of God that is waiting and welcoming? Do you know about his open arms and his waiting lap? Do you know about the part of God that agonizes over our hurting hearts and our broken spirits? Do you realize that on the night your parents split he cried more than you could ever cry and wept more than you might ever imagine?

He did. And he hurts for us.

The aching feeling of our parents' divorce can live inside us if we let it. And if we let it stay there, we become pain-filled and nasty. But now—right now—we have to surrender our pain. We've done that with our memories; we need to do that with our pain.

God wants us to surrender our pain, I think, because he knows if we hold on to it we begin to stink, and before long the pain becomes too much to handle.

THREE

RELEASE

THERE IS A SCENE IN an old Indiana Jones movie where this occultist priest locks unsuspecting people he intends to kill into a large, flat cage and begins chanting. The more he chants, the more his devoted followers, who are spectators to the whole event, chant, which turns into this huge emotional buildup. The more emotional the buildup, the more excitement, until at one point there is enough buildup for the priest's dramatic presentation. He reaches into the chest of one of the caged-up guys and pulls out his beating heart. The priest stands there, holding the guy's bloody and pumping heart. The guy who lost his heart looks at the priest, and then the priest looks at the heart, all proud of himself, like he's just made the world's best ham sandwich. The emotional tempo continues until ultimately the heart-less guy is dropped into a fire pit as a sacrifice to their god.

Wouldn't it be ludicrous if that guy whose heart was ripped out looked at the priest and said, "It's okay. Kill me. It's my fault for being in the way"? Or, if he said, "You want my heart for your occult ceremony? Okay. I feel angry about that, but I shouldn't feel guilty. It's your ceremony anyway. I'm just here watching."

Wouldn't he be the world's biggest idiot? Yeah. Because when someone's ripped your heart out, the last thing you want to do is take it graciously.

That's one of the real tragedies about divorce. We're often not allowed to express our anger. But, for the next few pages, we're going to do it anyway. There are some things we want to say to our parents, but for whatever reason we don't say them. Maybe our parents refuse to talk about the divorce or they are emotionally unstable, so our anger would only trigger further breakdowns. Perhaps we just don't have the guts. Perhaps we don't want to hear their answers. Or perhaps we don't yet feel strong enough to say these things out loud.

These next few pages are angst-y, so be prepared for some harsh words.

It's okay to be mad about our parents' divorce, and it's okay to express it. Getting this angst out is an important emotional release we need so that we can begin looking rationally at what's happening in our families. It's okay to feel these things, and it's okay to express them too.

Just a word of caution: Angst has its place. Being mad is okay, but it's not the end of our process. Let's get angry here at the beginning of our journey so that, by the time we're in the positive, hopeful part of this journey, we've felt the negative early so we can truly feel, understand, and internalize all of the emotions God has for us.

So let's vent.

Mom and Dad, How Could You Be So Selfish?

Here's how we look at your divorce: You couldn't hack it. You two don't get along anymore, and you fight, and you have different interests, and you don't feel in love, and so you've just chosen to give up. But look, when we're fighting with our brother, you tell us to be quiet and get along. When we don't feel like we love our sister, you tell us to act kind to her. And yet you've chosen to do something that goes against the things you've told us to do. Couldn't you have tried a lot harder to keep your marriage together?

You're being selfish, and it's stupid. What about letting the person you're married to get their own way? How about not having to get what you want all the time? Why do you feel like our identities and our family life are so worthless compared with what you think will bring you happiness?

Mom and Dad, Stop Treating Us Like Human Poker Chips

We're tired of you using us kids to get something you want from your former spouse. Like, for instance, when you want more money from Dad for whatever reason, and you know he has it but you also know he won't give it up unless you threaten him with something. And so you yank us into the whole problem with "Well then, maybe the kids don't need to come over anymore. How about that?" And you do that hoping he will give up the cash.

Or when you're pissed at Mom and you claim, "Sure. Okay. Look, you either do this, or I'm not going to show up to get the kids. See how you like it getting stuck with them all weekend."

We are not collateral, and it sucks knowing that you diminish our identities to that. Treating us like this is the worst thing you can do to us. Why do you think so little of us that you think we're a good bargaining tool? Do you hate your ex-spouse so much that you'd carelessly dent and damage us?

When you do that, it confuses our loyalty. Why should we love you when you clearly do not love us? How do we know who we should love? If you hate our other parent enough to threaten them with us, how do we love that other parent? How do we know about our own worth when you, the people we look to to find our worth, are so willing to give us up and use us?

Mom and Dad, Stop Making Us Choose Who to Love

We are tired of you putting us in situations where we have to decide which parent gets more of our love.

When you trash each other in front of us, when you treat each other like crap, when you make us decide whether our other parent is a good person or not, when you scream at each other on the phone, when you and your new spouse talk quietly about our other parent in front of us—those are moments when you're making us decide. Decode that for a moment: If you hate each other or act like you hate each other, when you treat each other hatefully, then we feel obligated, because we love you, to hate one or both of you too.

You have no right to do that to us. We love both of you. Both of you belong on a pedestal. Both of you belong in the center of our universe. We need to love you idealistically and realistically and passionately. And loving one parent does not mean that we don't love you too. It's okay for us to love both of you. Why are you so selfish?

Mom and Dad, Stop Making Us Keep Secrets

Here's the truth as we know it: If we talk to you about what we did at Dad's house, we know that a part of you will feel jealous, and honestly, it's easier just not to tell you. If we tell you about what Mom told us about the divorce, we know you'll get mad. If we talk to a friend, family member, or even a pastor—someone who cares—and you don't like it, we know we're in trouble.

Whatever is happening in our family is okay for us to talk about. It's okay for us to talk to each of you without fearing some kind of punishment from the other parent. It's okay for us to talk about the divorce to our friends without you getting angry. We need to talk. Let us.

Do you understand what's happening? If we can't talk about the divorce, what can we talk about? Look, the silence is killing us. It is pulling us apart on the inside. And that leads to us not knowing how we feel about much of anything. We can't talk about how we feel, so we stop feeling, and before long we just stop. Your secrecy is hurting us.

And above all of this, stop lying to us. Here's what a lie is: When you tell us something that's untrue about something our other parent did before the divorce, just so you think you'll look better to us, that's a lie. When you choose not to tell us the things you did to create the divorce, that's a lie. When you withhold facts about your relationship or stretch the truth about relationships you've had outside your marriage to out the other parent, that's a lie too.

Mom and Dad, Don't Make Us Grow Up All at Once

Do you realize what you're doing to our childhood? You're wiping it away, and here's how. You're making us learn things about the world before we're ready. You're making us deal with emotions we're not ready to deal with. You're making us face things that we're not capable of facing.

Okay, so we act like we can deal with them, and because you're so caught up in your own turmoil, you rely on that unconcerned exterior we're presenting. Here's the truth: Each time you make us face something we're not ready to deal with, we lose a little bit of our childhood. Each time we have to deal with these huge emotions, we light-speed our way through our childhood or adolescence and we miss stuff. We need to spend time feeling emotionally immature. We need to feel emotionally needy, and we need you to meet that need. We need to be our age, not the age we need to adopt so we can deal with your divorce.

Mom and Dad, Why Weren't We Enough?

Your kids love you and need you. You gave us life, and you teach us, and we rely on you. It's not easy being young. Truth is, we need you and long for you, and even if we don't always act like it, we want you around.

Why don't you feel the same way about us? You could have chosen to stay home just because home is where we are. You could have chosen not to divorce, because you knew how hurting we'd be because of what you did. You could have chosen not to be selfish. Why weren't we enough for you to stay home? Why wasn't our presence enough for you to endure whatever you felt you had to endure?

Here's how we feel now. If we weren't enough for you, we feel like we'll never be enough for anyone. We're going to constantly search for meaning because we meant so little to you. We're going to constantly feel like second-class people because we were not first class to you. We feel like dishrags. And what sucks is we know that you might remarry and you might start a new family and you might even have new kids. If we weren't enough for you when you were married to our other parent, will we be enough for you when you're remarried? We want to matter to you, and truth is, we often feel like we do not matter.

Mom and Dad, Let Us Be Angry

Here's how we feel when you tell us you're getting a divorce. We feel like we've just had an elephant dropped on us. We feel like we've been stabbed fifteen times with a dull, rusty knife. Our world is shattered. We know this is huge, and we immediately understand how life-changing this is.

So you need to let us react. We're going to slam things. We're going to yell. We're going to act out because we're hurting inside. Talking to us is wonderful, but just talking to us doesn't get rid of the anger we feel. Spending time with us helps, but it doesn't cover the pain we feel either. We want you to be good parents to us, and we want you to discipline us when our anger starts to hurt others, but still you need to let us feel and express this anger.

You've had your chance to get adjusted to this; we know that because you thought about your decision before you told us about it. You need to let us adjust. You need to let us be angry. And that will probably take more time than you would like or expect.

GOOD STAGES

Anger is important. Don't let guilt tell you that if you express anger you aren't a Christian. Much of our psychologically sensitive, overly spiritualized culture has adopted the idea that anger is unhealthy and that expressing it is never okay. Maybe our parents aren't comfortable with us being angry about what's happening. Too bad. Some people with confused ideas of what real emotion is may not be pleased when we express our anger. Too bad. Pastors or youth workers or other adults or friends sometimes tell us that anger isn't appropriate, for fear that we'll do something silly with that anger and use it to sin. Too bad.

There's nothing wrong with being angry and there's nothing wrong with feeling a wide range of emotions as a result of our parents' divorce. Check out the Gospels: Jesus laughs and cries and angrily flips over tables and makes accusations and fills his words with confrontational, sometimes hidden, rhetoric. Paul expresses love and joy and frustration and anger in his letters. Peter lived both frustration and joy. There is clear evidence throughout Scripture that you can both honor God and express anger.

But on top of that—if we really needed any more proof that anger isn't wrong—being angry is also psychologically healthy. Okay, so I'm not a psychologist and I don't have a degree in psychology, but you don't need a degree or a practice to know that emotions build up in us and need to be released. Counselors have thought through the place of anger in life and have realized that feeling and expressing our anger is essential to moving forward with our mental and emotional processing. In fact, anger is part of the grief process we feel when we're working our way out of our brokenness.

The stages of grief go something like this: The first thing we do when we experience the shock of divorce is deny it by imagining or acting like our parents aren't getting divorced. Next we get angry. Then we start bargaining with our parents and God. We say things like, "If I'm good, will you stay together?" When we realize that our bargaining won't work, we get depressed, and we live with that depression for either a short or a long time. When we've lived through that depression and when we've dealt with our other emotions, we come to that place where we accept our parents' divorce.

Without anger in that important series of stages we can never move forward. But I do think that when we're angry, it's important to consider what Scripture has to say about our anger, especially about how we express it. James cautions us to be slow to get angry (see James 1:19) and Paul warns us not to use our anger in a sinful way (see Ephesians 4:26). Being angry is okay, but we have to be cautious with our anger. It shouldn't lead us to sin. We should not live in anger. It's not okay to beat up our parents with our anger.

We should express our angst with honesty and gentleness. We can't compromise how we feel, but we don't have to be mean or violent in how we express it. We aren't the only ones who are hurting, and it's entirely possible for us to express our anger in such a way that it tramples all over someone else's expression of the emotion they're feeling.

The words we've expressed in this chapter are a good place for you to start dealing with your anger. If you want or need to say these things out loud to your parents, remember to do so with wisdom and respect. Think about what it means to express anger without sinning. And consider what it will take for you to move beyond your anger, because healing will never come if you don't.

FOUR

LOST QUESTIONS

INSECURITY SUCKS. YOU KNOW THE feeling, I bet. You want to be confident, but you really aren't. You want to walk through life with your chest out and your chin high. You want your confidence to enter the room before you, seep into the minds and personalities of the others in the room, take over the room with who you are. But it doesn't.

Insecurity can wreck you because, instead of living as the person God made you to be, it makes you always wonder if you're screwing things up. It picks at you, making you believe that you aren't who you think you are. It makes you believe that you suck just as bad as you think.

I have a theory about insecurity. Here it is. We have questions that arise as a natural result of our parents' divorce, and those questions are the very things that plant a seed of insecurity inside our spirits. That seed might sit for a while or it might sprout immediately. When it sprouts, that tiny insecurity plant grows and takes over. It chokes our soul and causes us to question and even deny God's love. It divides us from others who love us and who would seek to help us, if we'd let them.

Got a question that doesn't get answered?
Plant a seed.
Have an emotion you don't know how to handle?
Plant a seed.
Worried about your identity post-divorce? Confused about love? Feel emotionally lost?
Plant. Plant. Plant.

In our case, insecurity began when our parents divorced, but insecurity *explodes* inside us when we begin asking questions no one can really answer. These aren't the basic, run-of-the-mill kinds of questions either. They're the nagging, spirit-killing, insecurity-seed-planting kinds.

Below are some of the questions. While there aren't any quick or easy answers to these questions, we can begin to answer them together.

Who Am I?

We ask this question because our family defines who we are, and when our family changes, we change. I'm not sure that our divorced parents can really help us answer this question, because I bet they would say something like, "You're our kid. Your father's and my kid." But that kind of response requires both parents actually to be together. If they're not, then what kind of product are we? What if they openly hate each other?

So with that context gone, who are we? Are we still who we were before our parents divorced? So much changes . . . does who we are change too?

Here's the way I see it. Our identities become a new thing, a combination of who we were before our parents divorced and who we've become as a result of the divorce. You are still the person who loved to dance or listen to music or read or rent movies or hang out with friends. Your outside world has changed and your family context has changed, but that doesn't have to change your innate identity. You're still the person God created. You're still the person God made you to be, and your passion, personality, likes, and dislikes are all still in you.

Being the person after divorce means that you have to constantly remind yourself of your real identity. You have to tell yourself the truth about you. You have to remind yourself about who you are in practical terms and who you are as a child of God. So list those real identities. What are your likes and dislikes? Which of each parent's traits do you possess? Who are your best friends? What's your favorite thing to do when you're alone? What makes you laugh or cry? In what moments have you intensely felt God's presence? When have you known for certain that God was telling you to do something? What biblical character do you most relate to?

Is This My Fault?

As I've talked about my experiences with my parents' divorce, I've heard a lot of people express the feeling that they did something to cause the divorce. "Maybe I was too much of a handful and made them fight a lot." "Maybe Mom and I had too much fun, and Dad didn't feel like he was really a part of our family." "Maybe I asked for too much money." "Maybe my room was too messy."

Most of the time, before a divorce the parents are the grownups and the children are the kids. After a divorce, though, that often flip-flops. The parents are emotionally fragile and don't deal well with life after divorce. In many cases, they react the same way a child does—with crying, fits of anger, tantrums, the silent treatment, and so on. After the shock of seeing a parent react so childishly wears off, the child repeats the parent's behavior before the divorce. The child reasons, *When I hit my brother in the face, Mom comforted my brother and punished me.* So the child becomes the parent by comforting the hurting one and punishing the offender.

Once the child takes on the role of an adult, he tries to figure things out like an adult. By asking the question, "Is this my fault?" he tries in vain to fix it. The child thinks, *If I did something wrong, then I can do something right to fix it. Then my parents will be happy again and our family will be whole.*

It's natural to ask this question. And here's the truth: No, you did not cause this. Your parents were making relationship decisions before you were born, and they'll continue to make those decisions long after you've moved out of the house and built your own family. They made these choices and you had nothing to do with it. Even if one of your parents says their divorce was because you did something, they're wrong. Even if you did something really awful, you didn't cause their divorce. Our parents make their own decisions. This divorce was their own choice.

Am I Still Loved?

This question makes the most sense of all, doesn't it? Maybe the emotional math associated with the question goes like this: Our parents dreamed about us when they got married, and when we were born they both cared for us and changed our diapers and loved us. But now, if Mom and Dad share such vitriolic back-and-forth jabs aimed at each other, their hate for each other clearly translates into our understanding of their love for us. If they openly hate each other or if they're even violent toward each other, it's natural to ask if our parents still love us.

Maybe we ask this question because of a combination of two very natural things. First, we ask because of our need to be loved and cherished by our parents. And second, our parents need to provide for us and protect us, but sometimes their emotional response to their divorce or each other isn't so protective.

When our parents divorced, nothing about our loveableness changed. Our home environment changed, which changed our context, but our worth and value have not changed. So often when we're living through a divorce we begin to feel like we have no value, and that feeling makes sense. That structure that gave us a lot of our value has fallen apart and so has the certainty of our own value. And, you know, if we begin to internalize that feeling of not being lovable, we can make some pretty stupid decisions based on our negative feelings. But our worth and loveableness don't come from our parents in the first place; they come from our true Creator, who said he loves us unconditionally.

Does God Love Me?
God takes care of those he loves, but how can I believe he loves me? God could have made my parents stay together. God could have made them love each other madly. God could have made my childhood the stuff of Norman Rockwell paintings. But he didn't. Instead I had to grow up hurting, living with harsh realities that no child should ever be exposed to. If God loves me, why did he let this happen?

This is a question I struggle with to this day. When bad things happen in my life, I don't automatically turn to God for help. Deep down inside, I still question his love for me. God let my parents get divorced. God allowed me to get wrecked by their divorce. God couldn't love me, because if he did, my parents would have stayed together and I, well, I'd be that whole and together thing I was back before their split.

I am comforted, though, by the fact that our parents' divorce has not changed who God is. It has not changed how God sees us. Our loveability has not changed. See, this is the thing that is totally incomprehensible with our human minds. God, who does not change, also does not change his love. The power of his love does not change, the invasiveness of his love does not change, and the protection of his love does not change. His love is still his love, and anything that happens to us in our lives does not change his love for us.

Still, it's impossible to feel God's unconditional love when our lives are in turmoil. When you're not feeling God's love, it might help to find people who will tangibly express God's love to you. Pick a loyal friend. Hang out with your youth pastor. Go to your grandparents' house. Spend time with your best friend's parents or another significant adult. Put yourself dead center in another situation where you'll be constantly reminded of the fact that God's love for you has not changed.

IT'S OKAY TO ASK

In a divorced family, asking questions could possibly result in silence or in an outright refusal to engage—a huge NO. "Mom, why did Dad leave?" No answer. "Dad, please tell me what Mom did." "No." We are told over and over either explicitly or by inference that asking any question about what's happening is not okay. And that leaves us feeling like all questions are wrong, even the ones we feel desperate about or the ones we want very much to ask. But the fuel for those questions doesn't go away. That nagging insecurity doesn't leave. So we're left with an awful dilemma. We want to ask, and we want and need to express how we're feeling. But we can't. We're stuck.

When our parents refuse to answer questions, our mind goes in all kinds of crazy directions in search of the answers. Our mind starts putting together conversations we've overheard, situations we've observed, and experiences we've lived through, and it formulates an answer. The answer may be partially true. It may be distorted. Or it may be completely wrong. But if questions aren't allowed, we may come up with a more horrifying answer than the actual reality.

But I don't think we have to be stuck with not getting any answers. If your parents aren't talking and if your mind is racing to find reason, justification, or answers to what's happening, you don't have to settle. You can . . .

FIND SAFE PEOPLE

It's difficult to know who you can fire questions at. We have to be careful to ask people who can give good answers.

One group you could approach is your other relatives, but be careful, because talking to people who know the details of your family is tricky. Those relatives have a loyalty to the people they're related to in your family. But the benefit of talking with them is that they can offer you intimate details they've known about your family since before you were born.

Questions about what your parents were like before they were married and what your parents' marriage was like before you were born can easily be directed to these people because they have the best information. But be careful because their loyalties might prevent them from telling you the whole truth and their honesty might get them in trouble with their family.

You can also talk with pastors. It's important to have a spiritual counselor who can help guide your inner life anyway. Look for people who have a good relationship with and knowledge of God and understand his character as revealed in Scripture. They can provide a big-picture idea of what is happening inside you and inside your family. Most pastors who've been in the ministry for several years have counseled plenty of people with family difficulties, so they can advise you about how to live within your broken family.

The spiritual element pastors offer is something that most non-Christian counselors can't. You need that spiritual element because you're asking spiritual questions. Who am I? Am I loved? Answers to those questions that don't include the spiritual element aren't complete answers. Pastors can be that link between the head and the heart and the spiritual.

No matter whom you talk with, make sure it is someone safe who will sit and listen to you, who will cry with you, who will act on your behalf, and who will be the presence of Jesus in your life. These people have to be the kind of people who won't gossip about what you're asking. They should have deep knowledge of who you are, what your family is like, and what you're living through. Plus they also ought to have at least some life experience under their belt.

Use these people to give you that overall, well-rounded perspective to your questions.

RECORD THEIR ANSWERS

My four-year-old son is the best question-asker ever. He often stands in the center of the kitchen while I'm making dinner and pelts me with an assortment of *why* questions. "Daddy, why can't swidgerators fly?" and "Daddy, why are you a strong man?" And you know, I want to ignore a lot of his questions because they're often pretty silly. But the truth is, Jacob isn't really asking those questions because he thinks they're essential-to-life questions. What he's really asking is, "Dad, do you know everything? Will you share that with me?" Jacob not only needs to know that I know everything he needs to know, he also relies on me to offer advice about the stuff he doesn't know. He needs me to give up what I know because that's an essential element to the parent-child relationship. We need our parents to listen, and we need them to answer. When they do not answer, we're left to find out the things we need to know on our own.

Getting answers is important. Remembering those answers is essential, because those answers will give you more security than you could imagine. I know that if I don't write down answers to an important question, I forget them, no matter how important my question was. Write down the answers you hear and store them in a safe place.

NOT-BROKEN COMFORT

Parakletos is the word I spewed when I was at my first youth retreat.
I was uncomfortable being there because no one there really
spoke the way I thought normal people spoke.

During a Bible discussion at this retreat, we all sat in a meeting room. It really felt like a meeting, too, not an event or a fun
gathering or anything like that. We were kids, but we sat around
a conference table like we were approving a new product line.
The kids in that room seemed so strange. They had these perfect
Bibles with perfect edges—almost untouched. I didn't own a Bible.
They had really nice clothes and perfect hair. My hair was greasy
because I never really showered.

Anyway, *parakletos* is the word I used when the discussion
leader asked us, "What do you know about the Holy Spirit?" The
kids with the Bibles with the perfect edges and the washed hair
had a bunch of answers they'd been taught by their parents: "He
is God's Spirit" and "He gives tongues" and all the other stock
answers we often use when we really don't want to consider the
question we've been asked.

I guess my answer was pretty standard too, but no one in the
room knew Greek. My youth pastor had taught me some Greek—
well, he had taught me *parakletos* and that it means "comforter." No
one was really impressed by my use of the Greek language. And
no one really cared about what I said.

I may not have pronounced it exactly correct, but I think I get
points for being a kid and throwing around Greek. I was right,
though, because I now know for sure that the word is used in ref-
erence to the actions of the Holy Spirit. The apostle Paul uses it

to refer to those moments when we are in great distress and call out to God. When we do that, he brings comfort to us. He delivers that comfort to us through his Spirit. That makes the Holy Spirit the comfort deliverer.

I think that too often when we talk about comfort we talk about it like we're gathered around a conference table for a grown-up discussion or board meeting. But throughout the New Testament, God's Spirit isn't bridled and controlled. He is not neat and tidy. God's Spirit wrecked the first post-Crucifixion Pentecost in Acts 2. He disrupted the direction of the church with the conversion of Paul in Acts 9. He changed the mentality of the early church to include Gentiles in Acts 10. He changed people and hearts and minds. And along with all of that, God's Spirit comforted church leaders and answered lots of their questions. Paul knew that comfort and so did Timothy and Barnabas and Titus. God's comfort is not a controlled thing. It's clear that he gives it out. No, *gives* is too tame. Throws it out. Yeah, that's it. God throws comfort on us because he can't stand it that we're hurting or have nagging questions.

Jesus says it like this:

> "The Friend, the Holy Spirit whom the Father
> will send at my request, will make everything
> plain to you. He will remind you of all the
> things I have told you. I'm leaving you well and
> whole. That's my parting gift to you. Peace. I
> don't leave you the way you're used to being
> left—feeling abandoned, bereft. So don't be
> upset. Don't be distraught." (John 14:26-27)

FIVE

GOD AS PARENT

IT FEELS SO GOOD TO be wanted by your parents. It's wonderful when you realize that your parents don't just like you, they love you. And it's awesome to know that your parents don't just love you, they love being around you.

Even though they really love their kids, parents who are divorcing can become a bit emotionally distorted and do things that don't always work out the best for their kids. Those parents might be awesome, but divorce makes them not-so-awesome. Emotional turmoil strains even the best parent's ability to effectively parent their kids. Good parents become bad parents. All it takes is a not-so-simple divorce and all the stress that tramps in with it.

At thirteen, the courts gave me the option to choose who I wanted to live with. It was an easy choice for me: I wanted to live with my dad more than anything. I loved Mom, but I needed that dad influence. We talked, he was willing, and that was all I needed. I went home. I packed my stuff. I planned my move: what car we could use, where I'd sleep at his place. I looked forward to his cooking and his projects and the smell of his apartment. I looked forward to Dad.

Behind the scenes, lawyers worked with my parents, and together they came to an agreeable date when I could move. I don't know what happened in the interim between their decision and that date, but somehow, without any warning or any communication with me, the date came and went and I never moved.

I still have no idea what happened. Did Mom not want me to move? Did Dad? Who didn't want me? Who did? Was I rejected or was I clung to? Who won?

I remember asking Dad one night why I wasn't moving in with him. And this is the moment when Dad sat me down and began the process of using both hands to delicately crush my heart. He never really gave an explanation of why I didn't move, whether it was because of his or Mom's decision. But he was the one who had to break the news. He spoke as gently as he could, but still, all I remember is the feeling of suffocation while still being able to breathe.

Does God do this to us? Does he set us up with hope only to kick our teeth in at the last second? Does he make promises he has no intention to keep? Is God flawed like our parents? I've wondered about the kind of parent God is. I mean, if God walked the earth and had kids, what kind of parent would he have been? Would he be the parent who screams "No!" at his kids in the supermarket and the kind of parent who uses discipline and rules to keep his kids under control? Or would he be the kind of parent who loves his kids into obedience? Would God care at all about strict obedience? And I wonder if there would have ever come a point when God's wife would have said something like, "Look, honey. You're great and all, but it's a little tough being married to the kind of person who speaks things into existence. It gets a little old, if you know what I mean. Sorry, I'm checking out of this relationship. I'll be back later for my things." What kind of a parent would God be then? Would he be motivated by guilt and provide things and experiences because his wife chose to leave?

ASSOCIATION

This is the thing I have noticed about myself: Whatever I believe to be true about my parents turns into what I believe about God-as-Parent. If I believe that my parents are loving, then I will see God as loving. If I believe that my parents are not trustworthy, I will transfer that onto God and see him as untrustworthy. If my parents hate me, I will believe that God hates me. In some kind of cosmic way that I do not understand at all, my understanding of God is deeply entrenched into my own relationship with my parents. God and my parents are not the same, and yet I experience them in the same way.

Is God like my parents?

Houston, we have a problem.

If God and our parents are the same, that means God has bad days and good days. God can be moody. He can reject us so he can go on a date. God can get drunk and beat us. God could sleep with another woman behind our mom's back. God could duct tape us to a chair and whip us with an electrical cord until we understood his correction. God could say "I hate you" with his actions and "I love you" with his words. God could be a thermal blanket laced with glass and razor blades.

Truth is, God is not like our parents. Sometimes, in the best scenarios, our parents can reflect God. But God does not reflect our parents. He isn't like the dad who raised us. He's not like the mother who nurtured us. While our parents are supposed to be reflections of our heavenly Father, all parents fall short of Father God. And part of our broken journey is getting a grip on the kind of parent God is. If he isn't like our earthly parents, what is he really like?

Trying to quote Scripture about the kind of parent God is feels a little trite. Sometimes when Christians quote Scripture at each other, it often feels like we expect the Bible to solve all our problems. Sometimes we'll throw a Bible verse at someone, assuming that person will feel better immediately. Through experience, we know it doesn't work that way. But while quoting Scripture isn't a magic trick to heal wounds, it does teach us things— truths—which with God's help can gradually adjust our mindset and refocus our heart.

There is no escaping the fact that the character of God as Parent is all over the Bible. If we are to know the true character of God, we've got to find out what he says about himself and then see if his actions support what he says.

Here are a few of the ways that God reveals himself as Parent throughout Scripture.

Daddy

> For you did not receive a spirit that makes you a
> slave again to fear, but you received the Spirit of
> sonship. And by him we cry, "*Abba*, Father."
> (Romans 8:15, NIV)

Father is God's title, but *Abba* is the name his children get to use. Daddy God is accessible and loving and always there. This is the kind of Daddy who watches for us to see if we're coming up the walk after school, because he wants to know how our day went, or the kind of Daddy who longs for us to crawl into his lap when we've had a bad day. Abba is our ever-present reality and that kind of Dad who wants us to be with him all the time. I believe it was the Abba side of God that motivated him to send Jesus to die for us. Abba can't stand hurting or the separation of disconnectedness. Abba wants us so much that he would die for us.

This has been a tough one for me. Does God really want me on his lap? Or am I just the red-headed stepchild of the family—allowed in, but not really a part of the family? Can I take God at his word and accept the fact that he really does love me? God does not lie, so I know that he does not say things just to make us feel better, which means he must really want me around.

We can trust God and we can take him at his word. He is reliable and his reliability isn't stuck in his rhetoric. God does not just say he wants the best for us, like our parents sometimes say; his acts in our lives are always for our good. God doesn't just claim to love us; he acts lovingly, even to the point of offering himself for our rescue.

Abba considers us children, not stepchildren. *Full-blown children.* God wants to be with us, but not just when he has a few seconds. *All the time.* God wants to know about our hurts, but not just at the commercial break in the middle of his favorite TV show. *All our hurts.* God loves us, but not just when we're good. *God loves all of who we are.*

Disciplinarian

Abba is the love-side of God, but it is not the only side of God that we see in Scripture or that we experience. God gives boundaries because in his love he knows there are roads we should not take, for our own good. Those boundaries are all over the Bible. The Ten Commandments. The unusual laws in the Old Testament and the principles of love and other commands Jesus teaches. Each book of Scripture is filled with boundaries—and the consequences of crossing those boundaries.

Loving parents create boundaries; if God didn't love us, he'd have left boundaries out. It's that love-side of God that makes him willing to give us rules, even though we'll be annoyed and even mad about them. He gives us boundaries because he knows we'll hurt ourselves and probably others if we disobey. Like, don't covet, because if you do you'll end up killing to get what you think you need. Don't lie, because if you do you'll have to make up more lies and, in the end, you'll have created a mountain of lies to cover up that first lie and you'll lose yourself. Don't kill, because if you do you'll wreck other people's lives. Live love, because if you do you'll wonderfully affect everyone you meet and the people they meet and even the people those people meet.

God's discipline isn't warm and fuzzy. It's not something that is easy to go through. As a broken person I tend to react to God's discipline in one of two ways. I respond either with "See, I told you God hates me," or with "Who are you to tell me what to do?" It's part of that relearning process. God doesn't discipline in the same way our earthly fathers do. His correction is loving and firm. Just the way a good dad operates.

Proud Parent

> God looked over everything he had made; it was
> so good, so very good! It was evening, it was
> morning—Day Six. (Genesis 1:31)

Love and discipline aren't the only aspects of God that are important for us broken people. God is proud of us. Generally, he likes
who we are—the way we look and the way we smile. As a good
parent, he's proud because he sees himself in our countenance or
personality. And he is proud of our abilities. He is in love with our
laugh. He likes our intelligence. He is proud of us.

Look back to that passage in Genesis. At the end of creating, God sat back and said, "I am satisfied." When God said, "It
is good," he said it out loud. He told each part of his creation
how much he liked it individually. We see this as a part of his
character in the New Testament. Several times the Gospels
record God speaking from heaven saying of Jesus, "This is my
son, in whom I am well pleased." It was in God's character to tell
his son that he was pleased with him. It is in God's character to
tell us the same thing.

A vital part of knowing God as Parent is hearing him say to
you, "I am satisfied—with you!" God loves us when he looks at us.
He thinks, *Look at this person I've created. Isn't she beautiful? I love the person she is and the person she's becoming.* Our earthly parents know us,
and some of them aren't proud of us. God is not like that. He is
proud. He is ecstatic with who we are.

Doctor

God's parenting skills move outside the general parenting cate-
gories and not only into the part of him that longs to heal us, but
also into the part of him that has the ability to heal. Here's a story
that proves it.

> One of the meeting-place leaders named Jairus
> came. When he saw Jesus, he fell to his knees,
> beside himself as he begged, "My dear daughter
> is at death's door. Come and lay hands on her so
> she will get well and live." Jesus went with him,
> the whole crowd tagging along, pushing and
> jostling him.
>
> A woman who had suffered a condition of
> hemorrhaging for twelve years—a long succes-
> sion of physicians had treated her, and treated
> her badly, taking all her money and leaving her
> worse off than before—had heard about Jesus.
> She slipped in from behind and touched his
> robe. She was thinking to herself, "If I can put a
> finger on his robe, I can get well." The moment
> she did it, the flow of blood dried up. She could
> feel the change and knew her plague was over
> and done with.
>
> At the same moment, Jesus felt energy dis-
> charging from him. He turned around to the
> crowd and asked, "Who touched my robe?"
>
> His disciples said, "What are you talking
> about? With this crowd pushing and jostling

you, you're asking, 'Who touched me?' Dozens
have touched you!"

But he went on asking, looking around to
see who had done it. The woman, knowing what
had happened, knowing she was the one,
stepped up in fear and trembling, knelt before
him, and gave him the whole story.

Jesus said to her, "Daughter, you took a risk
of faith, and now you're healed and whole.
Live well, live blessed! Be healed of your
plague."

While he was still talking, some people came
from the leader's house and told him, "Your
daughter is dead. Why bother the Teacher any
more?"

Jesus overheard what they were talking
about and said to the leader, "Don't listen to
them; just trust me." (Mark 5:22-36)

Jesus healed because he chose to (Jairus's daughter) and
because he could (the woman). But he is not just *able* to heal; he
embodies healing. And because he embodies healing, all we have to
do is get close. Remember the woman? She just touched him and
she was healed. As I read that passage I am amazed that the event
created no fanfare, no marching band, no sirens or streamers or
confetti cannons. Had Jesus not turned around and acknowledged
the healing, we never would have known that, just by a touch,
Jesus healed this woman.

How many people got close enough to Jesus, were touched,

and walked away healed? We will never know. But I don't want to miss that opportunity myself.

Good parents take their hurting kid to get healed. God is that good parent. He knows our broken hearts and presents himself for touching. This is the God of the brokenhearted.

DOUGHNUTS AND JIMMY SWAGGART

Divorce left me feeling like a sad puppy that's always getting kicked. But as much as I felt this way, the truth is, I was not rejected. My parents were not devoid of love and good parenting. Here are some ways I know.

When I was a kid, I worked a paper route every Saturday. I threw about one hundred papers. It was a huge drag to get up, roll the papers, rubber-band them, load them into my paper bag, and then deliver one to each house. But the most memorable and best part about that route was my dad, who made Saturdays bearable by showing up at my mom's house and waiting for me to load his car with the papers. He would drive me to every house and help me deliver the papers. After delivering them, Dad took me to our favorite doughnut shop, and we would spend a lot of time talking and drinking coffee and eating doughnuts. As busy as his life was, he always took time to meet me and teach me.

And on many Sunday nights, Mom would move her sewing projects into the dining room, which was adjacent to our family den. She would sew, and I would watch Jimmy Swaggart, the televangelist. I loved watching him because he was full of emotion and feeling, and he was no-nonsense in the way he presented his beliefs. I didn't agree with much of anything he taught, but I liked the delivery and the emotion.

Really, what I liked most was the fact that when I watched, Mom was always in the other room, challenging aloud what he taught. Mom didn't agree with him, and she let me know about it. And sometimes when Jimmy was really teaching something she didn't agree with, the neighbors knew she didn't agree. I think one time the families three streets over heard about how much she didn't agree. But Mom never moved her sewing stuff out of that adjacent room, and on many Sunday nights she'd sit in that room and I'd sit in the den, and we'd watch and talk and be together. Mom was awesome because even though she could have let her despair take over her life and cause her to shut herself off from her kids, she didn't.

Looking back, I was not a kicked puppy. I was loved. But those good memories do not just quickly float into my mind. Usually the negative memories come first. If I stayed with those negative memories—the ones that usually come first—I'd be remembering a really wrong list of things, or I'd be remembering things about my past that were only half true. Only part of my own brokenness was negative. Other parts, things that happened during my parents' divorce, were very positive. Good stuff even happened in the midst of the divorce. And in many ways, my parents lived an example that was very much like Father God.

A lot of us want to stay only with our negative memories, or we spend a lot of time blaming our parents, or we even allow our remembrances of our parents to ruin our understanding of God. If you have a skewed understanding of who God is, one thing you can do is go back to those aisles of memories, pull out the good times you remember having with your parents, and write those down. Remember that your parents were not all bad.

And then spend time praising God for his list of revealed attributes. Praise him for the fact that he is your Parent, and he is perfect. And even if you can't find good memories of your parents anywhere in your memory warehouse, you've had a perfect Parent with you all along. It's good to tell God that you're thankful for him.

It's also good to thank God for those areas where our parents were or are exactly like Father God. Most of our moms and dads didn't *totally, 100 percent* mess everything up. They may have taught us that God always parents us; they showed us that by getting us up in the mornings and getting us to school and making sure there was always food to eat. They may have taught us that God always listens by taking time to hear about our day, even when their day was rotten. They may have showed us that God's discipline is right when they caught us lying to them and then leveled a just punishment on us. Sometimes our parents get it right.

■ ■ ■

It would probably be most comforting to end the chapter like this:

> One fine day, I discovered that I knew God so
> fully as my Parent that I understood completely
> who I was and I felt loved and whole and
> accepted. The end.

But the truth is, I believe this is a lifelong learning kind of thing. We spend a lifetime realizing and recognizing God as Parent. We spend a lifetime accepting God's parenting of us. We spend forever learning that God is the loving Abba and discipliner and pride-taker and healer. We learn and relearn who God is by living and experiencing. There is no pill we can take to completely understand God, and God does not drop understanding of him in a *kerplop* kind of way. We live with the knowledge that God loves us and seeks to reveal his parental nature to us. He does that because he loves us deeply and completely—more than our earthly parents could, whether married or divorced. And way more than we can comprehend.

SIX

SCABIES

WHEN MY FRIENDS AND I were kids, none of us believed that scabies were, in reality, skin-irritating mites that left annoying rashes. To us, scabies was a mysterious, coolness-killing disease that came from girls or from the really unpopular kid who always ate alone at lunch. One brush of the hand from any of those people and you'd get scabies, and if you got them, you were immediately stupid and you stunk and you couldn't play dodgeball very well anymore and you weren't any good at popping wheelies either. Scabies took whatever mojo you had and sucked it down into your rear end, where it stayed until you got unscabied. If you had scabies, it meant certain social death. Anyone who was thought to have scabies was instantly kicked out of any cool-guy thing. None of us ever talked about how we'd get unscabied either. The thought of getting them was bad enough. The thought of having to do something to get rid of them wasn't anything we dared to consider.

I was pretty good at avoiding scabies. Sure, other kids on the playground may have claimed that I had scabies, but they usually did so because they were jealous of my tetherball skills.

Yet my whole life I've felt like someone who has a bad case of scabies. I've felt like I have a disease that makes me so abnormal that I have no value for the human race. Scabied beyond hope. And when you feel like that, you'll do anything to feel better about who you are. Seriously. I understand people who drink, do drugs, or overeat because they feel like crap. If you've never felt awkward and strange and like you didn't fit, it's impossible to understand why people use substances to cover up those feelings.

People who say that God makes you feel better about who you are and that God will help you feel better about your parents' divorce too—I don't think they understand the actual way God makes changes in us. There often isn't an immediate change when one day you're scabied and the next day you're normal. The change that God brings happens over time. And so the change *out* of feeling like you have scabies takes a very long time.

I waited for God. I even became a Christian. I did the whole Christian thing. Surrendered myself. Went to Bible studies. Went to that youth group where we learned who begat whom and how sin affects all of us whether we like it or not. And when that wasn't enough, I enrolled in a small Christian college where God was readily available, like Band-Aids at a no-cost emergency room. And when we all sat in the required chapel services and my mind began to wander, memories about my parents' divorce and what I'd lost would invade my mind.

Depression became the only message I ever heard, and I became convinced that I was worthless. The depression I experienced felt so thick and murky that dealing with it seemed ridiculous, futile. Most often the despair I felt would come out during our neat and tidy chapel services. I would sit in those services and

imagine myself tying one end of a rope around my neck and the
other end to the brass pole that served as part of the balcony rail-
ing. I imagined throwing myself off the balcony and hanging right
there in front of everyone, just when the speaker with the
designer suit and well-crafted bio was hitting a high point in his
speech. I'd pin a note to my chest too—something like, "I'm that
scabied kid who's been sitting up here in the balcony waiting for
God to make me feel better. I give up. Send my stuff to my mom.
Thanks loads, Tim."

SELF-HATE

Self-esteem is something that people in the church debate about
a lot. Some people feel that self-esteem is incompatible with
Christianity because Christians are not supposed to esteem
themselves at all. Others, people who think like I do, I guess,
believe that liking who you are is pretty important. I believe that
you have to like who you are. I believe that, at least on some
level, you have to be satisfied with how you look and how you
act. I even believe that you have to find some level of satisfaction
with how you're living your life. I only say that because I've met
a ton of Christians who are so deep into denying themselves that
they don't care about things like quality of life or personal satisfaction. That doesn't make any sense to me. If God says he likes
us, but we don't like ourselves, then we are probably internally
confused. And while accepting God's love does not automatically
fix the problem of self-hate, we have to believe that getting to
the place of liking ourselves is something God wants and something that's possible.

Self-hate makes you feel always awkward. It's there under the surface, and it often dictates what you say, how you react, and most definitely how you feel. It shows up in the strangest places, like . . .

. . . When we're at school and we're standing at the end of the lunch line and trying to find that place in the room to sit. Self-hate tells us that no one in the room wants us to sit with them. We think no one wants to be our friend, and so throwing ourselves into our studies is the best thing we can do. Unless, of course, our self-hate tells us we're too stupid to make good grades, and then we're sunk.

. . . When we're with the opposite sex, and we're trying to feel natural and comfortable. If you don't like who you are, you don't feel worth their time or attention. If you feel you have little value, you'll probably make them feel that they have little value. And when either you or both of you are valueless, it makes stupid decision making easier. Sex becomes a defensive and Band-Aid response to feeling worthless.

. . . When we're at church, and we're trying to grasp the love and acceptance of God. It's easy to feel like junk in the midst of perfectly dressed people with seemingly perfect lives. If you feel like junk, how do you sing praises? If your mind rolls through a series of "you're the scum of the earth" thoughts each time you close your eyes, how do you pray? And what if you're actually honest with someone at church and tell them how awful and rotten you feel? Can you be that vulnerable? Is it safe?

. . . When we're alone, and there are no limits to where we can take our self-hate. Too often it turns into self-destruction. We smoke or drink excessively. We cut ourselves or find another way to hurt ourselves. We lie around because we feel deep within us that we have no real purpose. Being alone is the worst place for us self-haters because it's our privacy that allows our hate to become action.

Disliking ourselves so much often causes us to create little identity bridges between where we are right now and where we want to be. We imagine the person we can become, and we do our best to create a bridge to that imaginary person. We do that because we don't like us and imagine that if we can just be some-one else—someone we actually like—we'll finally be satisfied and happy and won't always feel so hopeless.

We create these bridges by checking the temperature on the outside of us. We look at who's popular, we consider who the cre-ative thinkers are, we study who is most listened to, and, most of all, we look around for those people we most admire. And then we create this mosaic like Dr. Frankenstein using choice body parts.

"That kid's popular, maybe I ought to get on the soccer team."

"That girl's cute, what if I wore my hair like that?"

"He seems happy, what if I hung out with that person?"

From each of those people we begin picking qualities we admire and transposing them into our lives. All of us do this to some extent. But when you do it to create who you are, what you're really doing is creating a pseudo-identity, becoming some-one you're not.

This is complex. We often dislike ourselves. We feel awkward. We don't know what we are, who we are—we have no sense of our own value. How do we "fix" this, as if "fixing" were the thing we needed? Do we just take a pill or drink some kind of magic potion or say some super-spiritual prayer and—poof—we're all better?

I think it's deeper and more meaningful and more pervasive

than that. I can't imagine that the change God makes in us from self-haters to self-lovers comes down to something as meaningless as being magically fixed by a trite, simple prayer. God's change has to be deeper than that.

But I want you to consider this: We know as humans that we have worth. We're made in the image of God, and God even sent his own Son to earth to rescue us. We know we're loved by God and we know God always seeks our good. So with that truth, how do we shed our scabies? We know being filled with self-hate isn't what God wants. How do we begin to move more toward feeling about ourselves the same way God feels about us?

BEGGING

We need to literally beg God for healing and hope and for a feeling that we are okay and not trash. I am not exaggerating or being melodramatic. And I'm not covering over all the emotion with a "just pray about it" answer.

Imagine it like this. We are starving. That's what self-hate really is. We starve for identity and for love and for our parents' attention and for the possibility of feeling normal and, well, insert that thing you're starving for right about here, because there's no end to the things that create this feeling of dissatisfaction. If we were hungry—hadn't eaten for days—and we walked past a bakery, wouldn't we beg the baker for some bread?

I would, just like I would also beg God if he were here carrying a bag labeled "Healing" or "Identity." It's okay to beg God for healing from our insecurities. And so, because I believe that begging God is okay, here is how I think we do that.

I believe we have to commit to deep, consistent, unending, regular, self-revealing, private times with God through prayer. In those times, pick something you often criticize about yourself that you want God to take charge of. You might hate the way you look, your laugh, your GPA. And then commit to telling God how much you hate that thing and beg him to either change it or help you like it.

Begging God also involves asking others to come along with us on this journey out of insecurity and self-doubt. It can be a pastor or a best friend or a parent. Tell that person what you're doing, ask that person to pray with and for you and to be willing to listen to your hurts and to have the guts to be honest with you and to step in if your journey gets stuck. Don't choose people who *say* they'll pray but don't. Don't choose people who *say* they'll keep in touch but won't. You need a physical person who really loves you and will commit to you.

LEARN WHOSE YOU ARE

It's easiest to associate our identities with our family, however it functions. But with divorce, we never know who we belong to. Although it's easiest to associate our identity with our family, *who we are* is bigger than our location, our parents, or our brokenness.

Plus there's a better question than "Who am I?" that is much more answerable: *"Whose* am I?" We are who we are because of who loves us. And that, by the way, is the same Person who created us, who knows us, and who unconditionally loves us. The question "Who am I?" is answered easily: "I am God's child."

The bridge to knowing our identities is this: We have to know what God thinks about who we are. And the Bible makes this position about who we are very clear. Here's just an intro to the many things God thinks about us:

- He calls us to him when we're too weak to live or exist on our own (see Matthew 11:28-30).
- Jesus chose to give his life as an atoning sacrifice for the sins that separate us from God (see John 19:16-30).
- God calls us his children, indicating that the barrier between God and humanity isn't just destroyed; we are made to be the actual children of God (see Galatians 3:26-29).
- God made humanity to be one, expressing love to each other as a mirror of his love for us, which indicates the breadth of God's love for humanity (see Ephesians 2:11-18).
- In love, he gives us gifts (see 1 Corinthians 12:27-31).
- God is pure, unconditional love, and he freely gives us that love (see 1 John 4:8-10).
- God encourages us to use the very personal name Abba when thinking about him and his relationship to us (see Romans 8:15-17).

Think of that list as our starting point. Our identity begins at the point of being lovingly created by God and then things assemble themselves according to God's plan. I am God's, so what am I like when I stress out? I am God's, so what am I like when I fall in love? I am God's, so what am I like when I'm standing alone in front of a lunchroom full of people I don't know? I am God's, so what will I be like when I move forward to career, marriage, and family life? Our connection to God feeds our identity and flows into all areas of our life.

Our Scabies Are Jesus' Marks

I don't know about you, but even though I know it's wrong to feel adrift on the "Who am I?" question, and even though I know it's wrong to dislike myself, those are two struggles that always seem to be right in front of me. I don't always know how to handle those, but I know where to begin my thinking about them.

Scripture is very clear about the identity of Jesus and how his identity refines and even protects our identities. We could probably quote lots of favorite Scriptures about Jesus, but I have one that fits here and helps us as we think about who we are.

> But the fact is, it was *our* pains he carried—
> > *our* disfigurements, all the things wrong with us.
> We thought he brought it on himself,
> > that God was punishing him for his own failures.
> But it was our sins that did that to him,
> > that ripped and tore and crushed him—*our sins!*
> He took the punishment, and that made us whole.
> > Through his bruises we get healed. (Isaiah 53:4-5)

Here's how this verse helps us. Jesus knows the pain of not knowing our real identities. He knows the pain of our failures. He knows what it feels like to be bruised. And those aren't just cognitive things; Jesus isn't just aware of all of that. Isaiah tells us that he's felt what we feel. Our pain over who we are becomes his pain. Our pain about not liking ourselves becomes his pain. He doesn't just know it all, he feels it all. And all that we've felt, he feels right now.

I have this bedtime ritual with my son. Each night I change him into his pajamas and we wrestle a bit. I read to him and we sing a few songs too. Without fail, Jacob will yell out, "Dad, do you got your eye on the monster?" as I'm leaving his room. I've never told Jacob about monsters and I have no idea where he got that idea. Still, the monster concept is deeply imbedded in his brain. It's the first thing he thinks about as I leave him. Maybe his four-year-old mind can't get past the idea that I've left him alone at the mercy of the monster he thinks waits patiently under his bed for that moment when I leave the room. I've always found it interesting that he doesn't ask if I can come back and kill the monster or if I would sleep with him to protect him from it. Monsters are part of his worldview. They exist. He just needs to know that I have my eye on it. So long as I am aware and watching, he's cool and he can sleep peacefully.

I find that I am the exact same way with God. Monsters are part of my worldview. The divorce. The pain. My awful scabies. My awkward feelings. They're a given. My words for God are a lot like Jacob's: "God? You there? Got your eye on the monsters? Okay. Cool. Good night."

There's a lot about God that I just can't grasp, and this is one of those things. Why are we often left with the pain, confusion, and self-hate after our parents' divorce? I am not sure. But I am comforted that it is completely out of God's character to take his eyes off those monsters.

FITTING IN

DIVORCE IS A LOT LIKE death. Because people don't know how to react to it or because they don't know what to say, people in your life get all weird. Many of them stop talking to you. And with Mom and Dad moving on and your friends not knowing how to talk to you, it's easy to end up feeling alone.

I don't think it's my parents' fault that I felt thrown out. It was all an honest reaction to the unnatural break of a spiritual union. When that union breaks, the fallout ends up rippling in directions no one can control and into the lives of several, sometimes many, innocent bystanders.

Community.

It's one of those things that gets totally affected when parents break up. No matter who we were before the divorce, we became someone completely different after it. And in the middle of the splitting, no one stopped to think, "Gee, I wonder what's happening." It all just happens and you just watch, like watching a car accident but being involved in the accident too. When the dust settles from our parents' divorce, everything feels fake-normal, like we become comfortable living with one less limb or without a vital organ. Doctors say that when you lose your sight, your hearing becomes more acute because your body compensates for that missing part. Maybe that's what happens to us in divorce. We're missing that important part and so we become more acutely aware of our other needs. We lose our family community and so we go looking for that missing part.

That's what I did. Naturally, both of my parents found new groups of friends. They were new, interesting, and different from what I was used to. My parents seemed to have made that important leap into new communities. I needed to do that, but I had no idea how.

OUR FAKE COMMUNITIES

Humans are tribal animals. We were created to be together and to help each other. Together in community we learn, rely on each other, support, protect, and share. The family is that tribe for all children whether they're from divorced families or not. We need that community because it is our safety net. It's our place of protection. It's also our social structure. Family is that organism that includes our parents, but also their friends and our friends and everyone connected to that unit. But sometimes community is found in different places, out of pure necessity.

I looked for community in a bike-racing group, but I never won any races and I was too scared to try any quality tricks. Down the street lived one of the cutest girls in our school, and so I tried to build community with her. Hanging out in her museum-like home meant being associated with the upper crust of the school, but she wasn't interested in me at all and my family was too poor for me to ever truly relate to her. Several blocks over were the computer guys. They'd sit and tinker with their Commodore 64s and make up simple computer games and play Dungeons & Dragons and things like that. They were the Star Trek guys who were quick to help you no matter what. Good-natured, but a little geeky. I was never smart enough to keep up with those guys. Before long I just flat gave up on trying to fit in, because I didn't seem to fit anywhere.

Eventually, I ended up fitting in with those kids who smoked pot. I enjoyed hanging out with them, but it had nothing to do with getting high. It was all about feeling accepted and loved and connected and safe—like community is supposed to feel. My teenage, pieced-together community could give the world the middle finger and mean it. They had good reason to be angry. One kid's dad was never home, so he raised himself. We never saw his dad, and I'm not sure he ever saw him either. His dad usually showed up long enough to buy his son beer (at least that's what my friend said). Another guy had good parents, but they didn't recognize that he was even alive half the time. They were divorced and often spent time using my friend as their go-between for their ongoing fights.

Our community meetings were fulfilling. We sat together. We talked and listened. We'd cuss and talk about the things we loved and hated. We laughed a lot over the stupidest things. It felt awesome to be in the middle of a group of people who had walked where I walked and who knew at a basic human level how hurting I was.

This was my community and my identity. We were throwaway kids, getting together because we had little or no stability at home, no accountability, and no enforced rules. We were each other's family.

And that was the key. Family.

It's not surprising that kids from divorced families go looking for significant people they can rely on who aren't their parents. In our society, each divorced family creates children searching for a new community. It's safe to say that when a mom and dad with two kids divorce, each of those four people finds a new community, creates their own, or hides.

Even around my "new family," I always felt like I was in community exile. Like I had done something wrong that excluded me from being a part of a "normal" community. Every relationship I had was temporary or was a "because" kind of relationship: I had friends *because* I needed them to make me feel some kind of normal. I was involved in things at school *because* I needed to occupy myself and keep myself from focusing on my family. But those were done as one who felt exiled from normal community and normal relationships.

Divorce created a me in exile. A nomadic teen searching for a group that would love him like his family was supposed to.

REAL COMMUNITY

There are pseudo-fixes which, to be honest, can be difficult to effectively put together. I mean, when you feel like you don't fit in any community, trying to assemble your own community is quite difficult. We often would rather tuck ourselves away than try to be a part of something, because being a part of something requires so much effort and vulnerability and honesty.

Finding new, real community has to begin with returning to our original context and our original family. Despite the divorce or the effects of it on us, we should always desire to reunite with our parents and do our best to somehow create community with them. Despite the fact that our siblings might have already created a community of their own apart from the family, we should also try to create community with our siblings. If either of those is an option for you, remember a few of the following things: First, remember that who you are as a family has changed. That means all of you are taking on new roles and possibly new identities. Your sister might not feel or react the same as when your parents were married. You're the same people, but you're possibly jaded or you're dealing with emotions you've never felt. In many ways, this makes you different people. Anything you establish now as a family needs to be talked about. You need to revisit as much about the divorce as you're able, and you need to discuss how each of you wants to be treated, respected as you move forward as a family.

Stop and consider the number of changes your family is experiencing through the divorce. Normal isn't normal anymore, and no one really knows the right thing to do, say, or feel. Because of the emotions your entire family community is feeling and because you're all experiencing a new family structure, remember that everyone deserves time to get adjusted. There's no set timeline for when you'll feel comfortable in this new community setup. Patience and grace ought to motivate each of you through this time.

To be honest, a lot of that feels very pie in the sky. Typical families don't hang together all that often, even when the parents stay married. So a family remaining in community after a divorce can, for some, be very difficult to imagine. Whether or not reconnecting as a family community is an option for you, you'll undoubtedly also find yourself needing an out-of-family community.

When you go out seeking that extrafamily community, remember that every community we attach ourselves to post-divorce should lead us to God. That means the focus, priority, and purpose of that community should be God. I'm not saying that the focus of that community ought to be church. I'm not against church, but not all communities that focus on church focus on God. Any community you become a part of should lead you to focusing your entire life on God. That community should refine your quest for God and should challenge you in your walk with God.

Good community encourages you to pursue the person God has made you to be. This good community helps you accomplish what you set out to do. It encourages you toward healthy living. It encourages you when you feel dragged under by the emotions connected with divorce.

Another way you know that you're living in healthy community is that those people know who you are. They're aware of your idiosyncrasies, and they like you. They celebrate those days that are important to you; they know your birthday. They love being with you. And they can tell just by looking at you when you're having a bad day. This is that caring side of your family that your family might not be able to provide.

Every healthy community expects things from its members. In other words, you can't just enter a community without giving anything back; that'll only drain the spirit out of the community. Good community offers you opportunities to make that community better. Being a good member means taking those opportunities.

Because we humans are primarily tribal in the way we long for community, we often will adopt ourselves into any community, even if that community damages us. It's a weird paradox: Because we're comfortable with the dysfunction of our home life, it can be easy for us to be a part of something that reminds us of our family. And sometimes we choose a community that damages us even worse than our parents' divorce did. We have to be careful that we evaluate our community within the scope of what is good and helpful, not the scope of what is comfortable.

LIVING IN EXILE

Being an Israelite in Old Testament times must have had its perks. So long as you obeyed God, you always had him on your side. As an Israelite, you had an entire history, complete with famous ancestors and important events in which your relatives or someone you knew had seen God's power. You had the history of God in the wilderness and the demonstration of God's protection and provision. Being an Israelite would probably have felt like you really were chosen and special. When you read the Old Testament, it quickly becomes clear that many of the Israelites *felt* like they were chosen. They acted chosen like snotty little president's kids who believe they can get away with anything.

It must have really stunk when the Israelite spiritual stronghold of Jerusalem was taken over by the Babylonians. I mean, you've got God on your side and then—*poof*—some foreign dude whose kingdom headquarters is a whole desert away from you and whose god isn't nearly as benevolent and protecting and, um, true as yours takes over your people and land. It must have been a slap

in the face. It had to sting when that Babylonian army beat the
Israelite army and sent them reeling into the desert. It had to hurt
when the Babylonians took Jerusalem captive and deported the
inhabitants to other cities, including places half a desert away.
With their spiritual headquarters under foreign occupation, the
Israelites must have felt awful, unhinged. With their families scat-
tered, they must have felt like homeless people.

It's amazing to watch God's hand in this story. I'm sure the
Israelites couldn't see God's hand in their loss to the Babylonians,
and I imagine that's why God comes and blatantly shows them.
He does that through the prophet Jeremiah, who gives us the text
of a letter he wrote to the exiled Israelites.

> This is GOD's Word on the subject: "As soon as
> Babylon's seventy years are up and not a day
> before, I'll show up and take care of you as I
> promised and bring you back home. I know
> what I'm doing. I have it all planned out—plans
> to take care of you, not abandon you, plans to
> give you the future you hope for.
>
> "When you call on me, when you come and
> pray to me, I'll listen.
>
> "When you come looking for me, you'll
> find me.
>
> "Yes, when you get serious about finding me
> and want it more than anything else, I'll make
> sure you won't be disappointed." GOD's Decree.
>
> "I'll turn things around for you. I'll bring you
> back from all the countries into which I drove

you"—GOD's Decree—"bring you home to the
place from which I sent you off into exile. You
can count on it." (Jeremiah 29:10-14)

Maybe the Israelites knew all the ins and outs of God, and
they understood that God could see their situation. Maybe they
already understood that God had their future taken care of. But I
suspect that *if* they knew, it was in a very cognitive way. They
knew all about it, but in this one moment they had to consider
more completely the protection of God and the plans of God.
They had to face their *belief* in God's plans. Did he really have his
eye on what was coming next for them? How could God really be
a protecting God, especially since they had been taken captive?

Where was God when the Israelites were sent into exile? The
letter proves where he was. He was watching, and in that watching he was protecting and ensuring the safety and futures of his
children.

If God was there when the Israelites went into exile from the
land they loved, then he was there when we were sent into exile
from the family we loved. God does not miss a thing. He sees the
divorce that sent us into captivity. He is already planning our rescue. He is already making a new home. He is present with us in
our pain. We feel forgotten, but that is certainly not what has
happened.

If we had a Jeremiah with us today, I imagine God would use
him to write a letter like this:

I know that this feels awful. I understand that
you feel lost and alone. I know this feels like the

worst kind of exile. I feel your disappointment. I
know you're sad.

But look. I am in control of this. I have this
whole thing assembled. I know you don't feel
like you can trust me in this, but you really can.
I'm sure you feel like I've turned my back on
you, but I haven't. I really haven't!

Hang on. We're going to go through some
white-knuckle weeks, but we're going through
this together. I'm going to carry you through
your parents' divorce. I am going to heal your
broken heart. I will give you a new community—one that you can rely on and trust, one
that won't break you.

Just stay with me. I love you too much to let
go of you. I am here with you right now. No
worries. Stay focused on me. This is a "we" thing.
We will make it.

God's words through Jeremiah are words for us broken people.
God has the entire picture in his hand. He knows what's coming
next for us, even when we have no idea. He knows our hearts and
the pain we're feeling. Most of all, he knows we feel nomadic and
stuck in a land without the community of our families.

Hold on. God sees, and he hasn't forgotten you.

EIGHT

DREAMS

I CAN MAKE UP MY own dreams. I can make them up even better than my mind can when it's deep in REM. Here is my favorite dream: My parents are divorced. Dad lives somewhere else, and Mom lives with us kids in our old house. Our life is happy and good. One day, Dad decides that he wants to come over for dinner. You know, to get reacquainted with the family. He calls Mom, who is eager to have him come over. They set the date—it's tonight.

We kids spend the day cleaning and making the house just so. We make our beds, vacuum, and mow the yard. We prepare for the reentrance of the King. We want him to be pleased and happy with his castle. So pleased that he can't help but stay. So happy with us that he can't ever leave us again. We love our King.

Mom works equally hard preparing a meal that will make the King realize that this castle is his *only* castle. There are mashed potatoes with creamy, brown gravy and green beans and hot buttered corn and cornbread stuffing. To top it all off, Mom has cooked the King a big, fat turkey. It's a little overcooked too, just like he likes it. The table is set like the picture she saw in a department-store magazine. The smell of baking apple pie hangs in the air.

Six o'clock. The doorbell rings. He's on time.

I open the door and the King reaches out for me with his warm hands. He picks me up and nuzzles his face into my cheek. My King feels so good and strong. My sister runs up to him and leaps into his other open arm from four feet away. He catches her, and the three of us hug and laugh and enjoy until my brother comes up, and then it's the three of us all nuzzling him and kissing his face and smelling his smell.

Our King is home.

We eat dinner and laugh all the way through. The King and his Queen touch and hold hands often. Once or twice, they kiss and look at each other the way married couples are supposed to look at each other, like they can't wait for the kids to go to bed. It's a good family time together—back together with our King.

And he likes us again too. We can tell; he looks each of us in the eye, indicating that he likes and respects us. He eats his pie quickly so he can read all those favorite old stories he used to read to us. He tucks us in and we fall asleep quickly because we feel good and safe. Our King is home.

And he really is home, because when we wake up in the morning he's there, in the kitchen, eating cereal and reading the paper. The next day he's outside mowing the lawn and trimming the bushes. And when we see him again that night, we know he's really sticking around, because he has the carburetor all in pieces in the driveway and his hands are greasy.

He *is* home.

This is the best dream ever.

After my parents divorced, all I ever wanted was for them to get back together. I dreamed about it a lot. I wished for it. I would have done anything to make it happen. I would have chewed my arm off, and I would have acted like I loved the feeling of having only one arm too. But that dream of Mom and Dad getting back together went on life support when they started dating other people. It officially died when they got remarried.

I didn't have any problem with my parents dating, so long as they were dating each other. I didn't care if they got remarried, so long as they got married to each other again.

Watching your parents date is like living in reverse. Dating happens before marriage. Marriage happens before sex. Sex happens before we are born. It feels unnatural to mix that order up. It feels wrong to see our parents go back to the things they did before we were born.

It feels wrong because it is wrong. We *should* feel that is wrong too. We weren't supposed to see them date. We weren't supposed to be a participant in their dating. It is unnatural, and it's okay to feel uncomfortable.

Here's the weirdest thing about parents dating. When our parents begin dating after their divorce, they often seem to be attracted to people who are totally unlike our other parent. For me, when my parents started dating other people, I wondered if their dating life wasn't more an attempt to prove to their former spouse that they could find someone better, prettier, stronger, or just different.

PARENT SELFISHNESS

Parents have emotional needs, and they have to be able to connect with the opposite sex. It seems fair that they should be

allowed to go out on dates. As a kid, a small part of me understood that my parents needed to date, but more of me—in fact,
almost all of me—saw dating as something they shouldn't do, at
least not very often. My parents belonged at home with me or at
work. If they went out with their friends, I didn't want it to be for
very long, because they needed to return to what was really
important. Each time they went out and didn't come home at a
time I was comfortable with, it was like I was rejected all over
again.

There are differences between the way parents see their
divorce and the way we think they see their divorce. When I was
younger, I always thought my parents' divorce really affected
them deeply and did so because the very fabric of the family was
pulled apart. But as I'm older now, I'm not sure many parents
truly see divorce as destructive to anyone but themselves. The
more I've reflected on my parents' divorce and the more I've listened to others' divorce stories, I've come to believe that a parent's first reaction to divorce is that they feel it is an affront to
their personality, character, and value as a human being. One
parent feels the marriage is preventing her from being all that
she can be; the other parent, the one who is shocked by the
divorce, sees the split as a slap in the face and an assault on his
identity.

Parents see divorce as an almost entirely personal issue, but
kids see it as a tearing and a ripping. This leads parents to believe
what is probably the most damaging thing they can believe about
divorce: that what's happening in the divorce only involves the
parents and doesn't involve or affect the children. While you and
I know that this is ridiculous, it's a very real belief.

LIFE SUPPORT

Both of my parents dated and remarried. For me, it was uneasy and difficult. Each dated people totally unlike the other and each ended up establishing lives completely different from the life they had when they were married to each other.

As they dated and remarried, I was in constant auto-protect mode. Honestly, if I could mentally or emotionally remove myself from their dating life I felt a lot better. So I just acted like I didn't care—but I really *did* care. I didn't want another Mom or another Dad, and I didn't need any more parents either.

Why is it okay for our parents to devote themselves to a new relationship when maybe if they'd devoted themselves to their former relationship we'd still have an intact home? Why do our parents choose to bail on their relationships only to form new and often equally flawed relationships?

Because they often don't consult us in their choices of dates or spouses, we have a decision to make. We can make their lives miserable and reject their dating and their dates, or we can commit to being flexible and adjust ourselves and our expectations to this new phase in our parents' lives. No matter what we might think about what our parents have done, we have to remember that they're still our parents. Their new spouses or dates deserve our respect because our parents do know them and trust them. In one sense we have to trust our parents' judgment. And we have to respect that our parents have taken the time to reinvest themselves in another relationship.

Sometimes our parents' divorce or remarriage makes us feel bitter, and we end up acting bitter toward them. Sometimes we get angry with our parents for divorcing and we take it out on the new spouse. However we feel about our parents dating, we have to accept that this is a new aspect to their new life. No, it's not fair. No, it's not natural. But for many of us, it's inevitable, and we have to continue to honor our parents through this awkward time.

Your parents need space to relearn how to have relationships. Remember, their last relationship ended unsuccessfully. Think of all the issues you face when considering going out on a date and multiply them—that's what your parents are facing. They want to look good, they want to say and do the right things, they want to be liked again by the opposite sex. They're struggling just like you'd struggle on a date.

New parents aren't easy-bake like macaroni and cheese dinners, and they're not always fun like a trip to the zoo. We hardly ever look forward to having them. We don't always find them easy. Regardless of whether our parents understand that, we need to communicate the fact that getting used to a new parent will take time. We need to prepare ourselves and ease into getting to know that new parent as the spouse of our natural parent.

That doesn't mean that if your new parent is abusive you need to put up with it. If your parent brings home someone abusive, the game completely changes. Then it's okay to disrupt, to call attention to the problem, and to take drastic measures to get yourself, and maybe your family, out of that situation.

JESUS GETS IT

Once your parents remarry, the secret dream of them getting back together begins to fade. The idea of a perfect marriage and perfect family is a myth, but it's a myth we can expect to possess. I believe we who are the product of divorce ought to expect our parents to stay married just because we've been born and just because we depend on them to raise us healthy and whole. And if our parents can't provide that, we should expect their new marriages to be stable. After all, they've had a second chance. Shouldn't this time be better and stronger and healthier?

Truth is—no. Mom and Dad are imperfect, and they'll make mistakes, even when they choose to remarry. We might get that perfect family when our parents remarry, but the chances are, we won't.

That moment when I realized my parents' marriage was really dead had to be one of those worst-moments-of-my-life moments. I'm not sure I can explain this right, but it was one of those desperate realizations where I was convinced that God could not understand or relate to me. How could God relate to any of this?

John, chapter 11. Jesus' best friend is in trouble. Bad trouble. Trouble like death. And Jesus is as cool and calm as he can be. His friends see that coolness and calmness, and they get mad about it. Mary's the worst because, even though she's seen Jesus' power, she still doesn't trust Jesus after Lazarus dies, because she's worried that Lazarus is too dead for Jesus to heal him.

But Jesus, being cool and all, takes the time to demonstrate what he thinks about what everyone else thinks about this, and about dead Lazarus, and about death in general too. Jesus says, "This sickness is not fatal. It will become an occasion to show God's glory by glorifying God's Son" (John 11:4).

I guess Jesus is supposed to say that. We expect him to do

something really holy and spiritual and God-glorifying. He's God—he's got the whole life and death thing covered. Dead people are no problem and sickness—really bad sickness—is no problem either. God's got the dead people thing covered.

Does he have the dead relationship thing covered too? How?

That question bothers you for about a nanosecond, because the best part of the story, the part I think helps us see Jesus' true reaction to the whole situation, is coming up next. We see Jesus being confident and secure here first. He lets those around him and even us see the theologically correct truth that he has dead things covered. And I guess that would have been enough, but there's a moment that we never miss but we also never stop to think about.

In the middle of all of that, even though Jesus knows he's the resurrection and has the power and knows his theology about all of this (in fact, he *is* the theology of all of this), he does something that moves this situation out of the realm of perfect, theological, and miraculous, and brings it into the real.

Jesus cries.

Who is he crying for? What's he *really* crying about? How loud does he cry? Why in the heck is he crying? He's God, so can't he, like, fix this? Which makes you wonder, Is this a helpless cry or another kind of cry? Maybe Jesus is just tired; he's healed too many people, and this one's gonna be a biggie. Too biggie?

It's a cry of sadness—that's what I think. Jesus' friend is dead and not only that, the dead guy has a family and friends, and those people are grieving over the loss. Their pain becomes Jesus' pain, and on top of the emotion Jesus feels for his friend, he feels the emotion of his friend's family. He weeps over the sadness he feels for his friend and the sadness he knows death brings.

So Jesus makes sure we get the theology, but he tops it off by weeping. That weeping is the connection to the real emotion we feel when we get that our parents will never be back together. If Jesus weeps over a physical death, certainly he weeps when we experience an emotional or relational death.

Jesus emotionally connects with that agony we feel when our parents' marriage dies. He gets it that we're aching. He doesn't just understand it in a comprehensive way; he feels agony along with us. He understands what it means to hurt. He gets what it's like to see someone or something you love die. He knows how bad our heart has ached and is aching, and he cries with us.

NINE

CHURCH PEOPLE

MAYBE CHURCH IS A KNEE-JERK reaction people have to pain. Is it like going to the doctor? For my family, if going to church every now and then made us feel better, my parents had no problem with it. But God was an ideology best left at church. There was no need to get radical and have it impact our life. We never really knew anyone whose life had been impacted and changed by God. Except, of course, those people we saw on TV, and they seemed a little crazy to us.

Church and God. Those two things become what many of us broken people look to. Some of us see them as lifesavers tossed for us when we're just above the surface of the water for our last breath. We need church and God, but not just because we need salvation. We need them because we need someone to sit and listen to us and cry when our pain is too evident.

My family began attending church before the divorce, which as it turned out was the best decision they had made since having kids. We became members of a church that had, among many other really good things, a strong desire to add people quickly to its membership rolls. You attend once and you're immediately added to the mailing list, and you become part of an exclusive club of people who meet in each other's homes for Bible studies and business meetings, and spend time lunching out and getting together on the weekends. Church was new to me and church people were new to me too.

Each Sunday, the pastor would hike up to the oak podium and talk theology I didn't understand about a God I'd never met. He'd usually use Charlie Brown or an example so dumb kids like me would get the point. Being there was important to me, and I'm still glad my parents chose to make church a regular addition to our life. Even if I didn't understand and even if our family never caught any of the theology we were supposed to catch, I knew that when I was there, I was doing something important.

Church taught me that religion, including God and worship and everything else like that, is beautiful. I knew this because behind the pews hung several twenty-foot-tall stained glass windows. They looked like huge paintings, made like God would have made them himself. Their characters were so detailed that it often appeared as if each pane of glass had been hand-painted by a famous artist. But they were not painted; they were constructed entirely from smaller pieces of glass, and if you got close to them, you could see each small piece.

Up close it was difficult to make sense of the theme of the windows. But looking at them from the pulpit, the stories the windows told made perfect sense. The life of Christ. Scenes of his teachings, miracles, death, and resurrection. They were grand and beautiful, and I knew that people who loved God and loved those windows were beautiful too. Church was a safe place with beautiful people.

For a time, it seemed like we were there a lot. We were there long enough to get to know a few people really well and long enough so that those people became part of the fabric of our lives. We were there long enough to have a few church socials in our home and for those good church people to come and see what kind of family we were. And they really knew us—at least some of them did. Some of them stuck around in our trying-to-be-normal life and saw what we were like. They were there when we were okay and together and the good church family.

But no one ever stopped by to see how our family was doing after the divorce. Back then, news about things like divorce spread like wildfire, and it couldn't have taken any time at all for word to get far enough around for some official at the church to know about it. But none of them stopped by to see what kind of people we were or what our values were or if we kids were demonic house-burning kids or good-natured kids who brought you lemonade and asked how your family was when you visited. Maybe all they needed from God was the cool windows and the silly cartoon stories so the gospel could be fun and comforting and easy.

That rejection made those windows feel like lies. Church felt like a memory stealer who didn't give a crap about how empty I felt. I loved God, but he didn't keep my parents from divorcing. I loved church, but they never checked in on us, even when they knew our family was splitting up.

This is the irony that church people sometimes offer to broken people like me. They suspend God in the air like a magically delicious, fix-a-lot kinda guy who always heals sores and fixes broken people and fixes them all in the same kind of way, making all fixed things exactly the same. Church people tend to offer God like doctors offer placebos. I think it's an inherent flaw in the typical Christian message that God will make you whole and heal everything in you the moment you accept Christ. And when God doesn't fix everything, we give him the benefit of the doubt, and we accept the blame for not getting fixed. We say to each other, "Oh, you must have unresolved sin," and so we send each other on a long internal search for all the things in us that must be preventing God's healing. And when we're still hurting, we are guilted into accepting more of the blame: "Maybe you've accepted Christ, but you haven't made him Lord," we say to each other. So we go on another long journey of giving things over to God and allowing Christ again to "sit on the throne of our hearts," all in an attempt to get this healing that we were promised when we became Christians.

But being a Christian doesn't mean being instantly healed and it doesn't mean being healed over the short term. I'm not sure I can explain this right, but I can try. I think some things are so damaging that they take time to unravel inside us. Like, if someone pushed a three-hundred-pound boulder down a mountain and the boulder was rolling at full speed, it'd take a lot for one person to stop that boulder. If the boulder was allowed to go all the way down to the city and crash into a few houses, the holes in the houses and the broken things wouldn't be fixed immediately. Damages would have to be assessed, and repairs would have to be planned, hired for, worked on, and painted over. It'd take a while.

So I'm wondering if our parents' divorce was a lot like that boulder. Just knowing the guy who fixes holes in houses isn't enough to have a fixed house. Maybe the damages in me have to be assessed and maybe things have to be worked out so that God can work the best healing in me.

FAKE CHURCH PEOPLE

Through the divorce and all the junk that happened in the wake of it, I clung to church. I didn't care that I considered it irrelevant, because I needed regularity way more than I needed relevance. I loved my church friends. But when I was with them, I always felt like I had to smile or not talk about how much I was hurting about my family. I had to smile like the paraplegic girl at youth group— severely broken, yet feeling like I had to mask my pain with a nice smile so people would feel more comfortable. I could talk about my pain, but people will listen only for so long before they tune you out or before your agony becomes too much and they change the subject. Showing brokenness somehow denied the saving work of Christ. Were I to show how broken I really was, I'd have had my salvation or sanity questioned. Pretending to be happy was the norm, and that's the way I had to live—in constant pre- tend mode.

It's easy to spot fake church people. They're the ones who walk past you and say, "How's it goin'?" When you respond, "Not the best today, thanks," they smile and keep walking. You can tell they're not interested and they don't care what's happening in your life.

They're also obvious with the kind of advice they offer. Those who tell you to shape up, pray, or weather the storm aren't reality-thinking people. They're saying whatever they can because they want you to keep moving and share your pain with someone else.

That makes those of us who are hurting *into* fake people, and that makes church the most confusing place to be when you're broken. You feel like you're constantly around fake people and yet you feel the pressure to be fake.

This hasn't always been my impression. I've met tons of awesome, caring people who loved me through my brokenness. Still, as a whole, church often feels too fake for me. And Christians? Well, it's easier to keep quiet about how hurting we are than to be open about it around them.

CHURCH AND GOD

Church and God are not the same thing. God, the Creator, Sustainer, and Lover of humanity, is open-armed and calls us to him. Church is that institution, the gathering of believers as a physical expression of salvation. God calls us together as believers to support and love each other in community. The purpose of the church is just that, but that's not exactly where the church always is in today's world.

God's aim for church isn't coldness or ineffectiveness. Acts 2:44-47 and 4:32-35 show us the intent of the first gatherings of believers. They care for each other. They share and give and encourage. What blows my mind is that in the Gospels, Jesus never gives any particular explanation about what he wants the church to act like as a "church." He never says, "Keep your theology all correct" or "Make sure you discuss your bylaws each year." His command was love, and his life was an example of that. So when you get to those descriptions in Acts where you read about how the early believers lived together in community, you see that their "church" was exactly that living love expression Jesus commanded.

Paul, whom God used to refine the conduct and beliefs of believers who gathered together in groups, offered all kinds of conduct ideas for gathering together. For instance,

> Live creatively, friends. If someone falls into sin, forgivingly restore him, saving your critical comments for yourself. You might be needing forgiveness before the day's out. Stoop down and reach out to those who are oppressed. Share their burdens, and so complete Christ's law. If you think you are too good for that, you are badly deceived. (Galatians 6:1-3)

and . . .

> The body we're talking about is Christ's body of chosen people. Each of us finds our meaning and function as a part of his body. But as a chopped-off finger or cut-off toe we wouldn't amount to much, would we? So since we find ourselves fashioned into all these excellently formed and marvelously functioning parts in Christ's body, let's just go ahead and be what we were made to be, without enviously or pridefully comparing ourselves with each other, or trying to be something we aren't. (Romans 12:5-6)

I could go on, but the clear call for us as believers is to walk through pain together. That kind of walking doesn't happen in the midst of people who live in an institution. We have to move beyond the structure of the church and get to the heart of who we are. Believers, called by God to gather together, have to be willing to listen, talk, and share their experiences. Not sharing is not being the body God calls us to be.

I carry a lot of bitterness about the church, and I think that's a result of my expectations. I have wanted and expected church to fix me. My disappointment with church is rooted in an anger that church was never there to care for my broken family, that church never stepped in to be God's fixing hands.

This takes a lot of relearning and, honestly, it means that we have to reevaluate what we ought to expect from the church. Despite God's design, the church doesn't always meet up with what he hopes the church will become. When it comes to the emotional and spiritual needs of us divorced kids, the church doesn't always meet us where we are. Can the church still meet our spiritual needs? Of course. Should we still continue being a part of a body of Christ? Definitely. But we have to re-create our expectations. Church isn't the perfect place where all people get immediately healed upon entering the building. Church is intended to be the expression of God's saving love in the world. It is an imperfect reflection of God.

THE NOT-MANIACAL GOD

So the math goes like this: Jesus came to show the way of love. He lived love and he taught love. The call of the follower of

Christ is to love in the way that he loved and to the extent that he loved.

Believers are called to this level of love, but the reality is that we often fall short. Churches, being gatherings of broken people, don't live up to this. It's a "yeah, we know what Jesus says . . . yada, yada, yada" kind of approach to living like Christ.

All of that, if you think about it, makes Jesus look maniacal, because he set an example for believers to follow that they never really will follow. Jesus, who could have made believers conduct themselves in a benevolent way toward broken people, did not do that. He left us to conduct ourselves on our own, and on our own we do a miserable job.

Where does God fit in to all of this? If church often does not connect with and properly care for kids of divorce, how does God connect with us? If church feels irrelevant, how is God relevant? We know God cares, but what is God doing in our broken situation in the first place?

I think that, along with getting a new grip on the role of the church in our lives, we also have to relearn the role of God in our parents' divorce. What's he doing in all of this in the first place?

Cue Gideon, the guy God approached to kick the Midianites out of his country. He was a chicken, but God called him "mighty warrior" (Judges 6:12). The guy who hid when God called. That guy. Chicken. The whole process from Gideon's call to the slaughter of the Midianites is amazing. God called the least likely person in the clan. God used him and a mere three-hundred-man army to take over the enemy. I wonder if Gideon was as amazed as he should have been.

Gideon beat that enemy using God's strategy. And what was

the strategy? Get a torch, put it in a pot, and, at the right moment, break the pot. The pot was hiding the torch, and in order for the torch to be effective for the battle, the pot had to be broken. The sound of the breaking would freak out the enemies, and the light released would fake them out.

God is clearly saying something about his call and about strategy in this story. Is he saying something about the power of broken pots? Whole pots were of no use to Gideon. It was part of the plan of God for the pot to be used as a whole thing and to be used as a broken thing. For those pots to be useful they had to be broken. The pot was essential to the process.

Here's another.

Jesus is about to be killed, although people don't know that yet. Things are probably pretty tense. Jesus is hanging out at a friend's house, and Mary, Martha's sister, brings to his feet a jar of expensive perfume, breaks the jar, and begins to pour it on his feet. The people in the room are freaking out. They want the perfume to be saved and sold to help the poor. I think they voiced their concern to try to impress Jesus. After all, he was the champion of the poor, so bringing up the poor to Jesus must have been thought to score brownie points. The odor of that perfume had to be strong. We're talking your rich grandmother's house after she's just had tea with thirty of her closest friends.

The point of this passage is clear. Mary's devotion and Mary's sacrifice. But the jar is also an important element. Without breaking the jar, all you've got is a nice gift suitable for shelf-sitting. The jar had to be broken for Mary to make her very important point.

The broken jar. The broken pot. That's us.

It is absolutely within the economy, plan, purpose, design,

will, and power of God for us to be broken. Maybe it's like this: In the Bible, things are dismantled and even broken for a purpose. Things are put into jars just so that whatever is in the jar can be released by breaking the jar. Brokenness exists in almost every page of the Bible. Moses was broken when God called him. For that matter, Jonah lived through brokenness during God's call. Job, broken. Paul, broken. Oh, and then there's Jesus. Broken beyond all possible comprehension. And broken for us.

Bitterness is the natural result of being broken. It's the natural result of the church never stepping in to be God's healing hand. Anger and frustration are only the beginning of the journey. The anger we feel is normal, but sticking with that anger and allowing it to become who we are isn't what God wants us to do with our brokenness. We can run to church and yell for healing, looking for people or situations that we expect to make us whole. But those people or places aren't necessarily the best places for our healing.

Inside us are the torch and the perfume. Light cracked through us when our parents divorced. Their divorce revealed something in us that lit up the planet. That smash of our jar released into the world a smell the world had never experienced. Without that cracking, no one would have ever experienced that perfume. And if that's true (and I think it is), maybe there's something really sweet or really important that's being revealed in us because of our parents' divorce. Even though we want to run to the church to get those cracks patched up and bandaged, maybe God wants those breaks and cracks there because something is going to happen in us as a result of those breaks.

Fixed? No, I don't think fixed. Fixed implies that there was no

TEN

COSTUMES

I LOVED SCARY COSTUMES WHEN I was a kid. I honestly can't tell you why or what my fascination was in making myself look scary or acting scary. Halloween wasn't my favorite time of the year, but I also can't say I didn't look forward to it. Usually, the discount store up the street would sell fake blood and fake scar kits. And sometimes I was able to convince Mom to buy me the fake blood and the Frankenstein scars and the werewolf hair and the vampire fangs too. It was not a fascination with evil or with a dark side; it was a love for dressing up like something I was not. Being Dracula and freaking out my sister was *awesome*. Being Frankenstein and growling like an angry mute guy at the neighbors was cool too.

There's something fun about dressing up as someone you're not, but while it was fun for a day to get in costume, I can't imagine being stuck play-acting like someone else, something scary, every day of my life. It would get really old. Who wants to spend their entire life like Frankenstein with their body full of electricity or like a mummy with pieces of them falling off all the time? That'd be a great Halloween, but it'd be an awful life.

I think this idea is pretty scary for kids whose parents are divorced. The scary part is the likelihood that we'll end up acting and reacting just like our parents. We're afraid we'll make the same mistakes they did. And the truth is, we *will* make mistakes based on all the inner pain we carry with us. We *will* wear our parents' divorce as a life costume, and we will walk and act like them. No matter what you do to not be like your dad, you will be like him. No matter how hard you try to not act like your mom, you will act like her. No matter how much you deny that you've been affected, you have. And the problem is, as much as you want to try not to repeat or react, you end up doing exactly that. Like a Halloween costume that really *isn't* you, you end up living like someone who is not you at all. And you live that way for the rest of your life.

Shedding that costume can feel impossible—it's something we desperately want to do, but we have no idea how. It's all itchy and hot inside there. I've often been scared that I'll repeat what Mom and Dad did, and repeat it unconsciously. I've often felt like I make decisions like Dad and Mom, not because I've consciously thought through those decisions, but because I'm conditioned to act and react like my parents. Their modeling always seems at the surface of who I am, with the me who wants to do good deeply buried under layers of hurt.

LOVE

The first time I saw the woman who would later be my wife, I knew I was in love. She was this smart girl from that perfect home I had always longed to grow up in. She was funny and interesting and very smart. Long story short: Her roommate was dating my roommate and the two of them didn't have cars, but Jacqui and I did. So at first it was a friendship based on being the third and fourth wheels, and it moved quickly from there and continued moving upward even after our roommates split. We fell in love and dated until I got up the guts to ask her dad if I could marry her.

Lots of people with divorced parents are afraid of marriage because of their parents' example, but for some reason, I wasn't. I figured marriage was a good fix, the thing that would solve everything. I knew other married guys, and none of them seemed to struggle with their identities. None of them seemed uncomfortable. I figured that if you're married, you don't struggle with looking at other women. If you're married, you will have more money. If you're married, you'll be happy all the time and you'll be starting out your life all new, and so nothing from your past will affect you. This is a new page, and you're writing a new story.

That kind of thinking doesn't last too long—about as long as it takes for that person you married to start doing the annoying thing your mom does or the mean thing your sister did. It's not too long before you're thinking this chick isn't as perfect as you thought she was.

Soon after we were married, I noticed I was repeating a lot of the same stuff my parents did when they were married. I made anger and disappointment the tone of my feelings for Jacqui, and I repeated as many of my parents' mistakes as I could.

I was awful, treating my wife like she was the queen of all the crap I had lived through. Somehow I had internalized the pain I felt from my childhood and that spewed out at times I could not predict and in ways I never expected. My awful husbanding dribbled into every area I was responsible for, including parenting our first child. My anger forced Jacqui to defend herself, which brought out the worst in her.

We lived this ongoing ping-pong relationship until one day when Jacqui and I were having it out in the car. We were yelling at each other and I was madder than mad and getting madder, and Jacqui was responding back with anger too. The whole time our child was sitting in the backseat and watching us fight. When Jacqui had yelled all she could and I had yelled all I could, there was this pause. And from the backseat came . . . nervous laughter. Tiny, like from a mouse. From that carefully strapped-in body and a mouth edged with leftover cookie came "Hee, hee. . . . Ha, ha, ha. Hee, hee, hee. . . ."

Did our toddler feel like she had to ease the tension?

And then came crying. Perhaps she was afraid that her nervous laughter made the two angry people angrier.

Did she really get what we were doing? She did. She understood everything.

It's one thing to know you're screwing things up; it's another thing to know how to make them right again.

How do we begin correcting this?

UNDERSTAND THE UNDERLYING EMOTIONS

Being broken means having broken emotions. And those broken emotions express themselves in broken and jagged ways. They tend to fly out at people we love and hurt them badly—even when that's not our normal identity.

I'm not an angry person. But once, in the middle of a huge fight with my wife, I did the only thing I could with the emotions that I was feeling. I took a baseball bat and I beat up a bowl of apples that Jacqui had placed, with pride, in the middle of our kitchen table. Then I demolished her favorite blue chair. Jacqui did what she had learned from her parents. She watched and cried. I know now that my anger was directly related to the rejection I felt as a result of the divorce. That anger was always just under the surface and was most probably fueled by the insecurity I felt.

I had pretty good reasons to be angry too: Confused about how to be a husband. Frustrated that we weren't living the good life I thought we deserved. Unable to figure out how I was supposed to fulfill all the commitments I had made up to that point. The emotions were deeper and more serious than anger, but they came out very angry.

At the time I had no idea what was happening inside me—I just felt angry. It would have been best if I had at least tried to evaluate what I was feeling and deal with all those underlying emotions. I should have dealt with my insecurity and my frustration. The first time I got angry and the first time I destroyed something should have been the clue that something ugly was happening.

Whatever is going on with us, whether it's anger in marriage or with friends, or whether it's bottled-up insecurity or self-destructive behavior, we all have to deal with the emotions going on inside of us if we want to try to avoid our parents' mistakes. We have to recognize that how we're acting is the direct result of how confused and disrupted we feel inside.

There are some questions we'll need to ask ourselves in order to think through our emotions:

- Why am I feeling this way?
- Why am I acting this way?
- What is the real emotion that I am feeling?
- What is the source of the emotion?
- How is this emotion coming out?

We also need to surround ourselves with people who will love us unconditionally and who will live with us through this emotional searching out. We need people to love us while we learn what fuels our negative emotions.

But we also need people who will teach us what healthy emotions really are. With the ongoing emotional dysfunction that is the inevitable result of divorce, even our understanding of what healthy emotions are is distorted. Looking for people who understand and live a healthy emotional life and who will willingly model that for us is an essential element in us not repeating our parents' mistakes.

LEARN THE RIGHT ACTIONS

Acting out in anger isn't the only inappropriate way we react to our deep emotions. We repeat other damaging actions, like keeping quiet when we should talk, hiding our feelings when we should express them, or pushing people away when we ought to allow them inside.

We do that instinctively. We do it because we're reacting to pain or simply because we watched our parents do it. When I was hurting, I kept secrets from Jacqui and wouldn't tell her how angry I was with her. This, by the way, conflicted with the way she was raised: Get everything out in the open immediately. In my house if you did that it meant that you didn't respect that person. In her house, doing that meant that you loved and respected that person enough to tell the truth immediately. I held hurt in, and when I let it out—oh boy, not good times.

When we fought, I always had in my mind that after each fight, one of us would have to pack their bags and move out. My parents never really fought like Jacqui and I did, but leaving or escaping from problems was definitely something I picked up from watching them. So for the first year of our marriage, I'd begin packing after fights. I figured it was over. I had to learn that fighting was not the end of our relationship. I had to learn that it was not okay to hold in my emotions. I had to learn that this deep anger was the result of watching my parents, and I needed to learn that those things I was living out were destroying my marriage.

Recognizing and learning about our deep-seated emotions helps preserve the relationships we've invested in, and it helps preserve relationships with those who are investing in us. Our spouses, best friends, girlfriends, and boyfriends all deserve that we not repeat our parents' mistakes. For the sake of our personal health and joy, and for the sake of our important relationships, we have to decide that we're not going to rely on how we were raised.

Some more questions to ask ourselves:

- Which of my parents' relationship-destroying actions am I repeating?
- What of their inappropriate parenting style am I repeating?
- What am I doing that is damaging myself?
- In what ways are my unhealthy actions affecting the people I love?

That lingering question "How does a healthy parent act?" was answered for me by finding, observing, and hanging out with parents who acted in healthy ways. While I'm sure that no parents always act right toward their children, it was important for me to find those who obviously acted in healthy ways most of the time. Because I had a mixed-up gauge of how to be married, I looked for examples of married people who were faithful to each other, paid attention to their kids, and were mentally and physically present with their kids.

FORGIVING MOM AND DAD

Here's the part of moving forward that I think tends to trip people up a bit. Sometimes it's easier to hold on to what our parents did than actually to give up that pain and forgive them. In fact, I've met a lot of people who seem fueled by blaming their parents. Their identities are soured with blame they won't let go of. I guess that makes sense. It seems easier to sit around and blame Mom and Dad than to forgive them.

But forgiveness opens up the door to freedom. For me, it's like this: When we hang on to what happened to us, we are locked back into that time and place when that thing happened. But forgiving them means letting go of that time, moment, age, period in life when our parents' mistakes hurt us.

The most important thing you can do here is talk to your parents. This means bringing up stuff that they might not want to remember, or definitely won't want to talk about. Talking to them means being very direct and knowing exactly what you want to talk to them about. It means knowing when to be persistent and to prod them with questions, and knowing when to let go for a bit and not ask some of the questions you really want to ask.

For you, talking with your parent about the divorce might not be possible. In many ways, this is true for me. But if it *is* possible for you to talk with one or both of them, it is ideal. Hearing our parents discuss that time is enormously helpful because it can connect those emotional and memory dots that we can't connect. Hearing them talk helps us sort through memories that are real versus memories that are a product of our imaginations.

If we can get our parents to discuss the events of the divorce, great. But not all of us can get them to talk. And the truth is, whether or not they're willing to discuss what happened to us in the past, we have to move forward. We have to forgive them. That forgiveness is a process; it doesn't happen immediately.

Two questions for you to think through:

- How can I forgive my parents?
- What do I need to forgive them for?

How do we forgive our parents? For some of us, it might just be a statement resulting from a discussion about the divorce, like, "Mom and Dad, whatever you did in the past is over, and I forgive you." For others, whether we're able to talk about the divorce or not, we might need to be more specific.

COMING CLEAN

Coming clean is the next thing we have to do in the process of avoiding our parents' fate. Like washing our hands before we perform open-heart surgery on ourselves, admitting things to God, right now, while we're alive, is the way to come clean about what we've done as a result of our parents' divorce. We need to admit our sin and pain and anger and humiliation and even our hatred of God—all of that. There's something about admitting things, even the hard things, that assures you that you're on the right path. I'm convinced that the process of admitting and confessing and accepting things fits the way God made us, and we have to do that whether we believe in God or not, because we're made to confess and admit.

Not easy stuff, because it's one thing to admit all the things Mom and Dad did that were wrong, but it's another thing to admit the things that we do wrong. We could lie and say that every wrong thing we do now is our parents' fault. But the honest way to come clean is to say Mom and Dad did things, and by doing those things I learned them, and by learning them I decided those things were okay. Admitting those effects is a killer. Sure, lots of those sins are adopted, but they're still mine.

Unless we confess the mistakes we're making, we can't make steps toward healing because we aren't aware of what needs to be healed. We can want to be clean and whole and even forgiven, but if we don't admit these things to ourselves, we'll just be traveling in circles. We'll just keep adding things to our secret lists of habits and mistakes that we've grown so comfortable with that they've become our identity.

We come clean by asking ourselves questions like these:

- How am I repeating my parents' mistakes?
- What of my brokenness have I adopted as my identity?
- How am I destroying my family or life because of what my parents did to me?

So obviously this is about understanding how we're living,

accepting that we're living wrong, and confessing it. Confessing our sin to God is important, but it's not the only confession we need to make. If we're married, we need to confess to our spouse the ways that we've adopted our parents' dysfunction. If we have kids, we need to confess to them the times we've been wrong. If we have other relationships damaged by our reaction to our parents' divorce, we need to confess to those folks as well. And in all these cases, we need to take real steps toward repentance by doing everything we can to avoid repeating the same mistakes again.

EMBRACING THEIR MISTAKES
AND MOVING FORWARD

There comes a moment in our brokenness when we have to forgive what happened in our past. This can be that moment. Getting a grip on our emotions is important, but we have to move past the blame. It's important to understand what the right actions are, but we have to move beyond the head knowledge and begin the right living.

Realize that what you lived through was not what God intended for you. Realize that how you were raised might have been completely different from the way God calls us to live. Understand that your parents made some bad decisions that affected you, and choose to forgive them. Confess what you've done that is wrong and then move on. Take important and intentional steps forward that promote healthy relationships and a healthy life.

Moving forward includes asking yourself,

- What of my parents' emotional damage am I continuing to hold on to?
- What healthy relational steps can I take today that are different from the unhealthy ones I took yesterday?
- What healthy parenting decisions can I make today that are different from the ones I made yesterday?
- What can I do today that will help heal the emotional pain I still feel?

Our goal as broken people is this: to not repeat our parents' divorce or the emotional turmoil that comes with it. The key to not repeating their mistakes is to move forward past what they've done and into what God calls us broken people to. He does have a unique plan for our relationships and marriages and parenting, and it's above and beyond the way we've been raised.

MUMMERS

Halloween. 1976. I was a mummer.

In my hometown, a mummer was a person, float, act, walking skit, or whatever else could not otherwise make it into the city Halloween parade. Mummers were the middle act in the typical multisection parade. They walked along, kinda sheepishly, kinda scared, and all of them knew they weren't good enough to be included in the more exclusive parts of the parade. Mummers did not stand on floats. They did not get special billing. No one really liked being a mummer, but no one wanted to opt out of the parade either.

Even though they were divorced, Mom and Dad worked together to make the most incredible pumpkin costume for me that our small city had ever seen. Dad fashioned the chicken-wire pumpkin frame and rigged internal lights to make the eyes and mouth light up. Mom used her expertise to make the best pumpkin-like cloth covering. I think I wore green tights, which was okay because it was part of the costume. And I walked that parade like I owned the mummer section—my pumpkin face all lit up and my green legs glowing under the lights of my pumpkin face. People pointed and waved at me. I waved back. I classed up that mummer section and made all of us with our homemade, barely pinned together, discount costumes look like parade royalty. I actually won a prize: Best in Class—Mummers.

When you think about it, we might end up mummering our way through life. Our parents made these costumes when they divorced. The costumes stuck to us and then, because we didn't know any better and because we'd been tricked into believing that we really like them, we wear those costumes our entire lives. In a very real way, we act out those costumes. We repeat. We reenact. We aren't *really* scary, but our costumes make us act that way. We aren't *really* that strange or damaging, but the costume makes us act and react that way.

Outside of God's design, we mummer our way through life, walking in the center of the parade in a costume our parents fashioned together out of who they were. And hey, some of us even wear them really well. We win awards. We present ourselves to the world just like our parents programmed us to. We look like we think we're supposed to look. We treat others like we were taught. We live broken because that's our costume.

But I need to tell you that this is not God's design. I can say this with absolute certainty. God does not like that costume our parents made for us. That costume can too easily become our destiny. We fight because our parents fought. We sin because our parents sinned. We cheat or divorce or do something far worse because we saw our parents do that.

God's desire for us is this: We have been created to be our own person, and until we shed that nasty, stinky, awkward costume, we will never be what he designed us to be. We have to shed the way we were raised. We have to put him on. I'm reminded of two passages where Paul says this:

> Rather, clothe yourselves with the Lord Jesus
> Christ, and do not think about how to gratify the
> desires of the sinful nature. (Romans 13:14, NIV)

and ...

> Therefore, if anyone is in Christ, he is a new
> creation; the old has gone, the new has come!
> (2 Corinthians 5:17, NIV)

So it seems we have an alternative. We can repeat our parents' mistakes *or* we can clothe ourselves with Jesus. We have the option to live like the new creation God is making us into. It's kind of a no-brainer.

This process of removing that old way of knowing and living is long and painful. It means relearning and rediscovering basic things: how to treat people we love, how to deal with anger, how to express emotions in healthy ways, how to stick with our promises. But those challenges from Paul aren't empty.

He offers them because he knows that God stands with us when we attempt to live like the new person he created us to be. We're used to the costume, so it might be difficult to part with, but we can take it off. And it will be worth it, by the grace of God.

■ ■ ■

It's after Halloween now. At least around our house it is. And my wife just returned from the discount store where she says she picked up some great costumes for next year. I had to tell her, "Honey, we don't wear costumes anymore." Nope, not the pirate hat. Not the fake, gross teeth or the cape or even the long, black, stringy hair or the scary mask. No Draculas or Frankensteins.

We don't need costumes in our house. Not anymore.

ELEVEN

HEALING

BROKEN ISN'T JUST YOUR FAMILY or the event that shaped you. Broken is your identity. What are you like? Broken. What do you do for fun? Broken things. Where do you go to relax? Broken places. The experience of your parents' divorce can be so pervasive and so hurtful that everything you are becomes a subtle exposition of and reaction to that event.

That makes healing sound really silly.

Silly because everything in us feels broken.

Silly because nothing feels like it will ever be right or fixed or healed.

Silly because there's still that kid in us who is more than hurt over what happened. We're able to keep that kid silent so no one can see him, but on the inside, that kid is still there feeling hurt.

I know healing is a good thing, but long after the whole event, and deep into life, I sometimes wonder if healing is a realistic goal. Can that kid inside us ever feel good or happy again?

Once I had this dream and in it I met an amazing kid. Throughout my dream this kid and I did all kinds of things together. We played and we talked and we ate ice cream. And this kid—he was just amazing. He was smart and he was so good-looking and he told the funniest jokes. I've known a lot of kids, but this kid was cooler than any kid I'd ever met.

In the last part of the dream, the kid and I were sitting on a huge rock, just talking, and I remember saying, "You're the greatest kid I've ever met. Do you realize how cool you are? I've loved hanging out with you. Who do you belong to? Do you have a home somewhere I can visit?"

And the kid looked at me and said, "I'm you, stupid. When you were a kid."

And then I woke up.

I always assumed that the dream I had was this message from God about the kid inside me who's stuck being a kid. Sometimes it feels like there's this kid inside me who makes decisions for me. It's not like he rules my life or makes me do things I don't want to do. This kid, though, sometimes he surfaces. Like . . .

. . . When I see something I want at the store, the impulsive kid inside reaches to buy that thing, and I can't stop him.

. . . When someone says something to me that hurts my feelings, my reaction is either to get really angry and yell or ignore that person and imagine that I don't have to talk to or listen to them.

. . . When I can't decide what to do with my life, the kid inside looks for a parental figure to put life together for me. Sometimes it doesn't matter who is around, the kid will listen to and obey the loudest, most authoritative voice.

. . . When Mom or Dad calls, that kid sometimes uses a really adult-sounding voice on the phone and tries to use bigger words because then Mom or Dad will understand that we have things under control.

. . . When the kid and I watch something on television about moms and dads, we often cry together, because we both know what we lost.

That kid in there—I'm not sure he's even supposed to be there. I don't think most people have a child trapped inside them. Am I the only one? There are days when that kid rules me, and at the end of the day I look back and see a bunch of stupid decisions. Yet I can't stop that kid. There are other days when that kid stays in check and Adult Tim is in control. Some days it's a mix.

Where did this kid come from? How did he get in there?

My best answer to myself is that when Mom and Dad split, part of me got stuck at the age I was when they split. For that matter, I imagine I got stuck at several significant stages, all related to really traumatic events. This makes sense, because most psychologists acknowledge that a child doesn't just feel the divorce, deal with the effects, and then—whammo—the child is better. Instead the effects of divorce continue throughout a child's life, up to at least three decades after the divorce. So maybe there are lots of little kids inside me. And maybe they're in there crying and needing attention, needing an adult to help them understand why they're stuck there. They need someone to help them understand why they haven't grown up.

The kids in me need someone to heal them.

I know that in the whole scheme of the healing process, any healing I might try to do on my own amounts to not very much. I know that God can do more healing in me than I could ever do myself. Still I tend to want to do the healing. I think that's because if we are doing the work, we'll feel like something is actually happening in our soul. And when we feel that much pain, we'll do anything, including taking over our own healing. If I can do it myself, maybe I can speed up the process and I can feel better sooner.

Can I make myself whole? Is it possible to even be made into a complete person? No, but it feels better when I try. Can I make my parents like each other? No, but it feels better when I try. Can I get my family back together? No, but it'd feel better if I could force them to stand in the same room for five minutes without fighting.

We can't do this by ourselves.

We need Jesus.

We need him in this because any of our own attempts to Band-Aid or fix will ultimately fail. They fail because this healing has to go to the core of everyone involved in divorce, way beyond our reach. It has to go toward our parents' own brokenness. It has to heal at the center of our siblings. It has to heal us too. And I imagine we need healing in places we never thought we did, and we need healing in ways we never imagined. I know I'm usually ready to get others fixed before I'm ready to get myself fixed. And usually I'm the one who's more broken.

Run, sprint, drive fast, back flip, crawl fast—do whatever it takes to get yourself into the presence of Christ because that is priority number one in our journey out of brokenness.

MEET THAT KID

Healing continues with meeting that stuck kid inside of us. And doing that means we have to go back, again, through those layers of our life and search for him or her. At whatever age we know we're stuck, we have to go back to that place to re-meet that kid.

This might mean going back to where you grew up. Maybe it means talking with someone who knew you then and asking them to tell you what you were like. It might mean getting a parent who will discuss the divorce to tell you what life was like then. Possibly you'll have to just sit and remember, and write down what you remember. Finding that kid might mean finding old pictures or old videotapes so you can see who you were then.

And when you've found that kid, these things help:

- Get to know the kid. That's you. Do you like him? Are you amazed at his creativity? Do you like his personality? Is he fun? Silly?
- Understand the kid. She's stuck there inside you for a reason. Who is she? And why is she there?
- Get inside his head. How does he feel about what's happening in your family? Does he know what's happening? How is he dealing with what he's living through? What is he feeling that he's not talking about?

Take everything you've learned and remembered about yourself back then. Imagine yourself praying and asking God to heal that kid inside you. Like this: "Jesus, this is me when I was nine. The night I discovered my parents were splitting for the first time. He needs a smooch and about five minutes on your lap."

And . . .

"Jesus, this is me when I was thirteen and felt so alone and missed my parents being married and felt like my parents had forgotten who I was. This thirteen-year-old feels lost and abandoned. I'm not sure how you can help here."

And . . .

"Jesus, this is me when I was fifteen and discovered that my parents were dating other people. He feels rejected. Could you get him some ice cream and tell him he's special?"

And . . .

"Jesus, this is me when . . ."

Is doing that too psychobabbly froo-froo-ish for you? I hope not. I like to think about Jesus as that guy who waits and heals for a living. He just sits there, maybe in a rocking chair all country and easygoing like, and he waits for us to get up the guts to ask him for a rock in the chair with him. And when he says yes, that moment is a holy moment like when you were created or when you die or when you first meet God.

Nuts and crazy? Nope. I know this because it says in Psalm 147:3, "He heals the heartbroken and bandages their wounds." God wants to meet that kid inside us. It's completely within his character to take hold of that kid, get out the Band-Aids and the ointment and the infection spray, and work to make our wounds go away. Healing is God's character.

CRY

Sorrow is entirely underrated. Sorrow, the act of expressing grief or the feeling of grief, gets a bad reputation today. Sometimes we feel that crying is showing weakness and that real Christians, if they're truly saved, would never feel sorrow or cry, especially over something like our parents divorcing. Sometimes getting confused and crying about our parents' divorce seems to mean we're somehow denying the healing work that Christ does. Really, nothing could be further from the truth.

Crying releases us from the need to hide the damage that divorce did to us. Crying reaches down to that place where the kid is and brings out all the emotion that's dragging us inward. Crying takes that emotion and makes it like an emotional prayer. The key here is this: You can't always cry alone. Too often, crying alone leads to desperation, which can lead into painful emotions that can cause us to do dangerous things. You need to find someone you're comfortable with and tell that person how hurt you are and ask him to sit with you while you cry. That other person with you is God's reminder that he is present and does love you. That other person isn't God, but is like God because he is taking the physical place of God. By the way, this is what it means to be God's hands and feet, which is one of the things Christians often say to each other. It's something we say when we want to be there for each other. Being present when others are hurting and letting them cry and hugging them while they do—that is being God's hands and feet.

Back when I hated myself in college, back when I wanted to kill myself, I felt stuck and desperate and completely lost. I pretty much latched on to my Freshman English teacher after she was vulnerable one day in class and expressed her frustration with God and talked about her own depression. Because I was feeling frustrated with God too, I made an appointment and we talked. Really, I talked and then cried, and then she talked and then cried, and I think hearing and seeing her cry was the most healing part of it. There's something about hearing someone else's anger and sadness and frustration that helps you deal with what you're facing.

Tears feel like a holy response to unholy pain. It's like crying works things out that can't otherwise be worked out through counseling or through talking to a friend or even through prayer. It is as if we have to cry so the pain has somewhere to go, and that somewhere is out of us.

I've met a lot of people who've talked to me about their parents' divorce and, like me, they've got these long stories about what they missed out on and what they wished for their childhood. I've asked a few of them if they've cried about all that yet, and they always look at me like I'm mental. "What? Me cry? No. Why?"

So I always say something like, "I'm not sure you can really understand what happened to you until you're crying about it. When you really get what happened and what you lost and what you missed out on, you're not feeling on the level you need to feel on. And when you get to that level; the only thing you can do is cry."

I've noticed that asking people if they've cried is a lot like asking, "Do you beat your dog?" People don't like thinking about themselves crying.

Crying is that last emotion. It's the emotion of desperation and pain. Feeling angry and violent and suicidal and hopeless and every other emotion—that is all a part of the healing process; those emotions all come out. But crying feels like that first emotion you feel when you're on the road back to being healed. For me, that's how I knew I was on that road God wanted me on.

TALK

Crying is the emotional reaction to the pain that's either buried or fresh, but it's not the only path toward healing. Crying gets out how bad you felt when your parents divorced, but it doesn't help you understand the event. Meeting the kid in you helps you reconnect with places where you feel stuck, but it doesn't necessarily help you process the specific tough times you experienced when you were younger. Talking is the rational side of this. It's the processing and expression of what you're hurting about.

The most important thing you can do in this step is to find a trustworthy person who will listen to you tirelessly. Like I mentioned before, when talking about the divorce with people, make sure they are safe and unwilling to tell others what you've told them. They have to be willing to listen and not share advice all the time. They have to be able to sit patiently while your verbal processing is sometimes mixed with tears. Finding this person can be a bit of an art. Pastors are a good choice, so long as you can find one who will listen without overly spiritualizing all your pain. Best friends are great too. Anyone who you know loves you and who will listen is an excellent choice.

When you feel damaged—a kind of damaged that doesn't seem to get resolved through talking with your best friend or your pastor or even through talking to God—you need to talk with someone professional who knows about how the mind works and who might be able to help you sort out your emotions. There's nothing wrong with talking with a counselor, psychologist, or psychiatrist. I haven't gone into that much detail about my own talks with professionals, but I've had them. Like about the time I opened up a pocketknife and threw it at this kid who was teasing me (had to see a psychologist) or about the time I tape-recorded myself calling Mom a really dirty name (had to see a counselor) or about the times I couldn't learn and Mom didn't know how to handle "Tim the hellion" (had to see psychiatrists). At the time I felt completely silly talking to a stranger about how I felt and why

I was acting so badly, but as I look back on those times, I'm convinced they were God-sent moments.

WRITE

Crying reaches that emotional part of you. Talking gets to that more rational part of you. But writing records it all. And for this journey, you need some things recorded.

When I first started journeying through my parents' divorce, everything came out emotionally. Like I said—severe anger, depression, and lots of crying. I didn't record any of the specific emotions I was feeling and I never wrote down the conversations I had with listeners. But there was this turning point when I actually started writing. First everything came out in poetry, mostly about how much I hated myself. Then very significant family events started coming out, and for the first time I started remembering things I had always known about but never really remembered. Before long, my anger poetry turned to hope, and after a while short sentences turned into actual paragraphs about my life. Writing is important because it works with us to remove layers of forgotten memories.

Writing is also important because it keeps a record of everything we're thinking and feeling and doing as we progress. We need that record of how we were feeling so we can see that how we're feeling today is really better than how we felt yesterday. We need to reread those moments when we were doing great so we can know that we'll feel good again. We need a record of those people who have meant something to us on our journey. Writing records those things for us.

I used to keep a small, black notebook. After a while, that changed to a black-and-white composition book. After that, I moved to the computer. Poetry, thoughts, hurts, joys, memories are all recorded there in different files. My hard drives have become my traveling journals.

THIS JOURNEY

This whole journey has to have some direction, and I think for each of us that direction is a little different. It's not like anyone ever really says, "Today you are on the path toward healing," or anything. And to be honest, I'm not entirely sure when I became aware that I was on the healing road God had led me to. There weren't any sonic booms, angels didn't start singing the "Hallelujah Chorus," and I didn't get any super powers or anything.

For me, there have been just little hints that show me I'm in the process of being healed. I think my marriage has been the best indicator of how far along in this process I am. At times my anger and depression and weirdness have created gulfs between my wife and me that seemed too deep and wide to cross. But there also are moments of redemption. Moments . . .

. . . When I look over at her when it's just she and I out for dinner. She doesn't have to speak—she just looks at me and I know what she's thinking and she knows what I'm thinking and we laugh. That's a connectedness they don't teach you about in premarital counseling.

. . . When we are both angry at the other and we tell each other so, but we don't yell or fight. We're just honest and we get it out, and afterward it feels like we did something huge.

. . . When she tells me how to drive, and I don't want to cuss at her.

. . . When we have family pictures taken and we both marvel that our three children are healthy and beautiful and stable and fun and funny, and we know that God did all that. And one of us catches the other's eye and we know how blessed we are.

. . . When she leaves me alone and when she can't leave me alone and when I don't want her to leave me alone, and she doesn't.

. . . When she brings me a cookie when I didn't ask her to, though I really wanted one. (She did that just now, and it made me cry.)

Like I've said, I don't completely understand how God's healing works. I know that God wants to make us *whole*. I know that we often use the word *fixed* when we're talking about being broken, but I don't think I like that word because it implies there's this perfect thing we all have to be like, the perfect human or perfect Christian or perfect representation of God Almighty. I don't believe in *fixed to be perfect*.

Whole implies what is truer about God. He is a Healer. He's a longing Healer, the kind of Healer who seeks us out and seeks to make us whole, like he created us to be in the first place.

And that's not fixed. I imagine it's something deeper, something that takes a lifetime.

TWELVE

STORIES

HERE'S A SECRET A LOT of us never understand about having a perfect family or creating a perfect family. Please prepare yourself because this fact will absolutely blow you away. You will wet your pants when you read this. Promise.

If you want a great idea of what the perfect family looks like, all you need to do is read the Bible. If you read either the Old or the New Testament, you'll discover how perfect families operate and treat each other. You'll see the perfect thing God desires, that perfect environment all of us broken people know we should have grown up in. There in those thin-as-onion-skin pages of your Bible, between Genesis and Revelation, are the best examples of husband and wife, sexual purity, perfect children, perfect fathers and mothers, healthy family relationships, and so on.

Because of that, all I really need to say here is this: If you'd only read your Bible more, you'd (1) understand what the best biblically based family is and (2) be able to live that family ideal in your life. And if you were unable to accomplish either 1 or 2, well, maybe you need to work on your spiritual life because anyone can see that God's people and their family relationships were perfect enough to model.

So go read your Bible and see what you missed out on . . . that perfect family and all.

I know that sounds ridiculous. I mean, I *hope* that sounds ridiculous, because it is. Sometimes it feels like we Christians want to promote this idea of the biblical family, the biblical family that is healthy and whole. We Christians have done an incredible job of sanitizing what the biblical family really is. And for a long time I thought the biblical family was that perfect kind of thing.

What a stinkin' lie.

When you take Scripture in its entirety, considering all the stories we have about all the people God introduces to us, the biblical family is about 70 percent messed up. Really, it's more like 90 percent, but I'm feeling generous. Here is a short list:

- Adam and Eve disagreed about the fruit and then screwed up everyone's life.
- Cain killed Abel.
- Both of Lot's daughters slept with him.
- Abraham played favorites between Ishmael and Isaac.
- Isaac played favorites between Jacob and Esau.
- Jacob played favorites between Joseph and his other sons.
- When Esther's parents died, her uncle made her sleep with the king.
- Saul tried to kill his son.
- David cheated on his wife with Bathsheba, and then killed her husband.
- Hosea married a prostitute (because God said) and then proceeded to name their kids things like "Unloved" and "Not my people" (because God said).

- We never hear about Mrs. Paul.
- Timothy came from a religiously mixed marriage, and we never hear about his father being the spiritual leader.

The biblical family is not at all perfect. It is probably a lot like that family you heard about whose dad is never home or has a few girlfriends on the side or whose kids are so messed up your mom won't let you play with them, even if you stay in the front yard where she can see you. We want so much to believe that there is a perfect, biblical family. We want to believe it because it means we have this perfect standard we can expect and work toward. If our homes were a wreck, at least we could rely on the biblical family model. But if there is no biblical model to work toward, we're a little lost. What hope is there for the families that we create?

We could not control the story that divorce created for us, but we can control the pages of our story that are being written today and the ones that will be written tomorrow. We can control the story that will be written about the families we create. We and our spouses and our children can write the best story. It can be a story of dramatic change, showing how the story we were raised in isn't anything like our story right now. We can change the story of our lives and write new plots and new chapters. Our lives can tell the story of healing in our past and hope for our future.

We can call our future anything we want. We can say, "We're breaking the chains of our family's divorce" or "We're relearning how to have a healthy family" or whatever. But the process of learning and healing and changing from our parents' divorce is different for each of us. We each have different issues and problems and experiences associated with our parents' divorce that are as unique as our fingerprints. This is our new story, and it's written on our lives by God. The story that defined us and our family in the past does not have to be the story that defines our future. Whatever and whoever has affected us in the past is not our entire story. There is more to be written.

Our future stories are really a combination of several smaller stories. Here are a few of the most important stories that have made up our past and that will frame our future.

OUR STORY OF GOD

The story of God in our lives began with our parents. They introduced us to God. They either told us he existed or they taught us that he didn't. If they taught us about the existence of God, they also exposed us to his character. From what our parents taught us, we learned about God's love, grace, and forgiveness, and all of God's other character traits. If our parents didn't explicitly teach us about God's character, they taught us by modeling those traits. And if they didn't model them or teach them to us, we learned about God by watching our parents. If our parents taught us that God was an angry man, that's how we imagine God. If our parents told us that God is loving and forgiving, we will carry that idea of God with us for the rest of our lives.

We don't always think through where our God-story came from. That's because the story began in us long before we were conscious of our parents' teaching, back when we just accepted everything our parents did and everything they taught us.

All of us have been taught or shown elements of God's identity and character. That's our God-story. What has yours been? What will your God-story be tomorrow?

In other words, in what ways is your understanding of God obviously distorted? Do you view God as an angry guy? Or too permissive?

To move forward and live the story of God in us for the rest of our lives, we must acquaint ourselves with who God is. We talked about only a small part of that in chapter 5, but we have to consider more than the parental revelation of God. We have to devote ourselves to reading Scripture and seeing God's true character in dealing with broken people; we have to learn what God is like when he's judging or forgiving or instructing. We have to learn about all that God is.

What has your story with God been so far? What will it be tomorrow?

OUR STORY OF OURSELVES

The story of who we are began when we were born into the home and to the parents who raised us. Our identity was shaped long before their divorce. The environment we were raised in provided our understanding of who we are. Sometimes we need a decoder to understand this correctly. If our parents loved and cherished and respected us, that definitely helped form our identity into something very positive. If our parents treated us like junk, that became our identity. Most often we don't stop and consider the extent to which our families have shaped our identities. Our home environment either was encouraging and nurturing or it damaged us. And because that's the environment we had known since we were born, we take the influences (whether they're positive or negative) for granted. We don't think about them.

The story of our identity can be tragic; it can be a story of the person who had great potential but has been wasting that potential for the past many years. Our story could also be one where we were raised in a terrible home but rose above the rotten place to live a changed life. See, the story of our identity is influenced by our families, but it's not controlled by our families.

You've been living an identity you inherited and learned from your family. What will the story of your identity be tomorrow?

OUR STORY OF REALITY

Our reality stories are often confusing and difficult to unpack. Here's the simplest way I can think of to understand our stories of reality.

Homes are like these tiny little worlds. When we were kids, we believed that everything that happened in that little world was true. We learned about others inside our home. We learned about the outside world from our home. We learned about truth and morality and everything else from our home. We learned what ideas are "right" and what words are okay to say and what beliefs are true or wrong. Home taught us what is true about the world and what is not true about the world.

If that tiny world was distorted, teaching us strange and untrue things, we still won't doubt the validity of what we were taught. If we were raised to believe that every adult other than our parents is evil, we will believe that. If we were raised to believe that loving parents always beat their kids, we will believe that, even though it's distorted. It does not matter what is really true; our home environment is truth.

If we've been raised sheltered or closed off from the real world, our story is limited and canned and too small. If your story has had a very limited cast of characters, what will your future story include? If your future story is to be healthy and well developed, it will include many people and many new ideas.

OUR STORY OF OUR FAMILY

The story of our family began when our parents married. Long before we were even thought of, our parents formed a relationship. They were the two lone characters in their developing story. But we and our brothers or sisters added to that story. We became part of an ongoing tale that we did not control.

Our family stories can be really strange, because there's that part of us that we let the outside world see and then there's the part of us we only reveal when we're home alone within the context of the only story we really know well.

Our *real* family culture isn't like the one we let others see. While all of us probably grew up in families where we always portrayed a good, healthy exterior, the reality inside our homes was probably different. Outside our homes we were constantly trying to be happy, but was that the true story of our family? Some of us have homes that portray themselves as carefree and fun, but the real story is that our homes are stress-filled and angry.

And of course, that family story obviously changes when our parents divorce. The story becomes something different. Before, our story could have been titled "Consistent" or "Unchanging," but now it could be called "Always Changing" and "Constant Movement." Our traditions change. Our stability changes.

Your story may be that your family life has been inconsistent or broken or damaging. What will your future family story be?

OUR NEW STORY

We tell a lot of stories in our home. In fact, storytimes are some of our most memorable times together. At night, just as the kids are settling into bed, we'll get together and recall either a moment the kids want to remember or a trip they've almost forgotten. Many times they'll ask for a scary story; I've got loads of good scary stories. I tell them about a relative who, at night, unzips the skin on the back of his head so he can let his skull breathe. Or the one about the neighbors who have fifth appendages we can't see. You know you've got a good story going when the kids run screaming from the room and almost pee their jammies.

Our best storytimes are the ones when we all get involved in the story. I start by trying to make this great creative beginning, one that my kids can easily take in all kinds of directions. And then Nicole, my oldest, steps in to continue the story. She takes the story in the direction that she thinks is the most interesting, and that direction is usually very intricate and highly developed. After Nicole has told her part of the story, my middle child, Jessica, takes over. Jess always goes for the laugh and often will create a situation or a character that gets us all rolling. Jacob sometimes joins in. He's so very young that his additions don't always make a lot of sense. He often borrows a lot of what we three have already said, and sometimes his additions include wild things like flying people and the man who had macaroni for hair and forks for hands. Jacob's best addition to our stories is the enthusiastic "Yay!" he always adds at the end, indicating his joy at being part of the process.

My kids love being a part of our make-up story nights. And them creating stories with me is exactly how our lives should be lived.

This next part of your story—the part that is living itself out in front of you from this moment on—is an incredible journey. It does not have to include divorce or hopelessness or brokenness. This next part is the story you choose to live. See, to some extent, we get to be in charge of our stories. We choose to live broken and we choose to live healed and we choose to live the adventure. We choose to turn ourselves over to God and allow him to write our stories.

If you're not currently looking forward, it's time to set your eyes to the future. There is more to your story. There are more characters to meet, more locations to visit, and more plots to uncover. As broken people, we can choose to look back on the stories that used to define us or we can look forward to the story that God has yet to write. Looking back means depression and hopelessness and wallowing in pity and despair. Looking forward means adventure and hope and healing.

Our stories should end with a "Yay!"—the excitement that comes from allowing God to write and direct our future.

Today is a new page for us. God has begun writing our new chapter.

It's good to know that God loves a good story.

GOD'S FULL CIRCLE

GOD IS FUNNY, BUT NOT ha-ha funny. He's weird and strange and interesting funny. God begins things in us and then leaves them alone in us to see what happens. Healing works that way, I think. And for me, this book has been that process of God planting the seed and then leaving it alone to watch what that seed would do in me. Do I cultivate it? Let it die? Eat it?

I committed myself to write this book more than fifteen years ago, before I was married, before I understood healing, and before I grasped how truly broken I was. I wanted to put something together that would help someone else survive this brokenness. When we were first married, my wife and I invested in our first computer for the purpose of me writing a book that would help other kids of divorce. I wrote and wrote and, after a while, the seed lay dormant. Friends helped edit, people prodded me with ideas, and I read books and gave talks about divorce and all that. Every few years the idea of putting together a book like this surfaced; the seed sprouted a little bit more, and before long it became a plant.

Through that time I changed: My understanding of the grandeur and power and presence of God grew, my own personal spiritual quest dismantled and reformed itself over and over, and even my marriage went through different seasons of growth and death. Through the process, I've learned about God's timing. There comes a point, I believe, when God takes what he has planted in us, pulls it out of our ground, and replants it or exposes it in such a way that others see what he has done or is doing. This book has been that divinely planted thing in me. Fifteen years ago I was not ready. Ten years ago I was pious. Five years ago I was a wreck. Today I am squarely on that journey toward God and toward healing.

This is our life journey. It continues now. It continues forever.

Reliving the moments that have shaped me into who I am has been quite a journey. It's been difficult knowing what events to include in this book and what advice I've picked up along the way to include. Of course, I've left a lot of things out. My family moved a few times, once across country. There were people who entered and exited our family structure. There were family parties where I learned some karate from one of my parents' friends, and there were many happy Christmas mornings and lots of good times.

Almost all of the experiences I've talked about in *Broken* happened in Ohio, where we moved when I was about eight. My identity struggles, my parents' dating, and almost everything else I've mentioned in this book occurred in that small Ohio town, mostly in our family home. You know how kids remember their old homes as a lot bigger than they really were? Well, this place really was big. High ceilings and a large basement and one huge walk-in storage room that had a floor lined with newspapers from the 1930s. We lived and loved in that home until Mom remarried and sold the place. I went to college. Mom and my sister went to their new home. My brother had moved to an art college a few years earlier. We sold that place twenty-two years ago and, in selling it, we surrendered many of our dreams and memories.

In the final days of completing the first draft of this book, I was back in Ohio on vacation with my wife and our three kids. We had planned to take a few hours one day to show the children around the city where I grew up, hoping that seeing where I was as a child would help them know more about their dad.

We pulled up across the street from my old home and noticed that it was for sale; there was to be an open house the next day. So we returned the following day and, with the permission of the real estate agent, walked around the house.

The place had not changed. After more than twenty years the carpet was the same, the wallpaper was untouched, and the marks we had made in different spots were still there. It was as if time had stopped: I was twenty years older and returning home for a quick visit.

The open house lasted two hours, and no other family or buyer showed up to preview the house. As we walked from upstairs all the way down to the basement and back up and down a couple more times, we noticed that this moment seemed like a tiny gift from God. Maybe God was celebrating the fact that I was actually going to finish this book. Maybe God was teaching me that, despite how changed I felt about my parents' divorce, going home is still possible. But maybe God had something different in mind.

Upstairs, in the room where my sister used to sleep and play with dolls and escape me when I was chasing and teasing her, hung a sign left by the previous owners: "Tough times don't last. Tough people do." I'm not sure I believe that God sends us physical messages. I don't believe in reading tea leaves to discover the heart of God, and I'm not into omens or divine signals or anything like that. However, that moment in that empty house was a moment when I believe God spoke.

Maybe he was saying something like, "This pain does not last. But I do, Tim. Stick with this. You're going to be okay." Maybe surviving life isn't about being tough. Maybe lasting through divorce is about leaning into God's chest and enjoying his toughness for as long as we're able.

So as I pondered that little divine surprise, our family wandered around the house a bit more and then out to the backyard. And again, believe it or not, there was another word, scribbled on a sheet of poster board leaning against a wall just outside the house. It said, "Remember." That concept, an anthem for divorced kids, was God's reminder to me to continue walking the house, to do my best to reach back for those memories and to embrace them. It's okay to remember. It's okay to lean into God's chest. It's okay to go home again. Remembering is not easy, but it is the best thing for us broken people.

Being broken doesn't have to mean being inept, insecure, scared, or unstable. We will always be broken, but we do not have to *live* broken. We are cradled in God's hand. He loves us, calls us to remember, and urges us to rely on him. He lovingly heals those broken parts he wants healed, and he listens and cares when our broken parts hurt us too much. He's the best daddy we could ever have.

I don't know how you feel about being broken, but I know how I feel. Some days I feel awful. Some days I feel okay.

However I feel, Abba Father is right there, reminding me to hang in there and keep going. I know he wants me to deal with my brokenness and do my best to be the person he created me to be. I understand that being broken is not exactly what he wanted for me. But as much as I can, I rely on the truth that God issues an unending call to climb up, sit on his lap, and tell him how I'm feeling. My Abba loves me up there right in his face, and he loves me telling and confessing and crying and resting in him.

God loves us even when we sit in his lap, kicking and screaming. He loves us when we sit there and blame him for all this pain. He loves us when we take his healing for granted and even when we deny his healing and his help. He loves us when we've sat there long enough and finally realized that what we really need is him and his healing and his hope.

He loves us, and he longs for us to come home.

ABOUT THE AUTHOR

TIM BAKER IS THE STUDENT Ministries Director at Hope Fellowship and author of fifteen books, including two Gold Medallion nominees and one Gold Medallion winner. He currently lives in East Texas with his wife, Jacqui, and their three children.

LEARN TO GET REAL WITH GOD AND YOURSELF.

Redefining Life: Identity

1-57683-828-5

There is freedom in knowing who you are, and this discussion guide will help with the process. You'll not only discover what you were created for but also learn about the One who created you.

Redefining Life: Relationships

1-57683-888-9

There are no easy answers when it comes to relationships. But you can develop strong, godly habits to prevent relationship drama before it begins. Learn how you can be a better friend, roommate, boyfriend, or girlfriend with this practical, advice-filled book.

NAVPRESS
BRINGING TRUTH TO LIFE
www.navpress.com

THINK

Visit your local Christian bookstore,
call NavPress at 1-800-366-7788, or log on to www.navpress.com
to purchase.

To locate a Christian bookstore near you,
call 1-800-991-7747.